Broken Cisterns

By

Francis W. Schaffer

Copyright © 2003 by Francis W. Schaffer

Broken Cisterns
by Francis W. Schaffer

Printed in the United States of America

ISBN 1-594671-20-6

All rights reserved. No part of this publication may be reproduced or transmitted in any form or by any means without written permission of the author.

Unless otherwise indicated, Bible quotations are taken from the HOLY BIBLE NEW INTERNATIONAL VERSION. NIV©. Copyright © 1973, 1978, 1984 by International Bible Society. Used by permission of Zondervan Publishing House.

"NIV" and New International Version" are trademarks registered in the United States Patent and Trademark Office by International Bible Society. Use of either trademark requires the permission of the International Bible Society.

Xulon Press
www.XulonPress.com

Xulon Press books are available in bookstores everywhere, and on the Web at www.XulonPress.com.

Dedication

To believers in Jesus Christ everywhere that are having their "nests stirred," longing for renewal in the Church.

Contents

Dedication v
Introduction ix
1 / Questioning the Church 15
2 / Desperation for God 21
3 / Looking for the Power of God 29
4 / Forsaking Niagara...35
5 / The People of God 43
6 / The Same Heart and Love 55
7 / A City Wide Church 61
8 / The Work of the Holy Spirit............................73
9 / Misplaced Gifts 95
10 / Ministries for Everyone 105
11 / The Path 115
12 / The Meeting 137

Introduction

This is a book of observations. As I pour over Church history, I see very little resemblance between the power-filled Church of the first century A.D. and today's Christendom. The true Church was born through the resurrection of Jesus Christ and the outpouring of the Holy Spirit for the purpose of proclaiming God's glory to the earth. Since the first century, there is a sure pattern, past, present and future; the Church has been profoundly affected by the world rather than vice versa.

The body of Christ is to be exactly that, His body on the earth, doing the things He did and *"greater things than these" (John 14:12)* because He went back to His Father. He came and conquered and left the rest to His redeemed bride led by the Holy Spirit. Everywhere the Church is there should be peace, for we carry in us the means of reconciliation; there should be conflict, for Jesus said that the world would hate us for loving Him; there should be great victory, for in Him we are more than conquerors because He loved us. But the world goes on as it always has; aimless and lost. It is our responsibility to be at work with Him to bring the message. We are to work as individuals, yes, but more than anything, over the time since the fall of man, He has been trying to establish a people called by His name, organically alive, functioning together, inadequate alone, seeing the earth come to learn Christ.

The church has been like a group of Lone Rangers. We admire his independence, he was a loner. When the frontier town was helpless against bank robbers or cattle rustlers, our hero would ride to the rescue and deliverer the people without getting dirty and seldom would he even lose his hat. The only one who got any credit other than the Masked Man was Tonto and he was presented as merely a "sidekick."

If God had written the story line, it would have been reversed. The town would have come to the aid of "Kemo Sabe." God deals with peoples not just persons.

Moses was called by God not to be a hero of the people but to be a servant of the people. God used Him to establish Israel as a people to show His glory to the earth. David was to be King over the nation. His responsibility to God was in how they prospered with him as King. The list goes on; Samuel, Daniel, Isaiah, the Twelve, Paul and Timothy all were meant to build a nation to show God's character, qualities and countenance.

The American concept of rugged individualism flies in the face of the biblical call to submission and it is submission that will build a holy nation. In American Christianity, humility, service and dependence are words seldom understood or included in our conversations. They are qualities that must become prominent in the Church in order to overcome this individualism.

Christianity needs to not just be a subculture that functions apart from lost America but a counterculture. We are to walk in the world the way Jesus did, ministering while still being untouched by it. Can we be something that we have never been and never seen? Can we be something that seems so foreign to us?

The American Church must think in corporate terms when studying and meditating on scripture. We must ask: "What is God saying to us?" Up to this time we have asked: "What is God saying to me?"

We have missed the point of God's gifts to the Church. The gifts that the Holy Spirit gives to each believer are for the body, not just the individual Christian. They are for the betterment and edification of the Church not just the Christian. God has uniquely designed us as individuals to fit into the whole and function dependently, fruitful not only as one but as many. He has also brought us together geographically and culturally not to be complete in ourselves but to fit into the larger context of a city-wide and regional Church. It is my contention that the religious systems that we have built have done much to discourage and very little to encourage this godly plan.

Where is the power? The words, *"signs, miracles and wonders,"* are used throughout the book of Acts to describe what God was doing through the faithful. Why are we so different from the Church of the first century? If that was the birth of the Church then where should we be two thousand years later? Far too many people are saved and then live with many of the same problems and habits that were part of their life before their salvation. Where is the transformation? Something is keeping us from seeing all that God intends His Church to be.

Do we need to dismantle the religious systems that encourage denominationalism, racism, gender inequities, generational differences and overall unfruitfulness? If so, then can the Church ever get free of the cultural and traditional confines of religion - what we have decided will please God? Only in crying out to a Holy and Forgiving God and asking Him to establish us in His order and purpose will anything change. Only if we are willing to obey at all costs.

Could we have been the victims of error, passed down from generation to generation; error believed for so long that it has become "our truth"? Could we have lived with it so long that we can't even recognize it? Have we detached the truth of the Word of God from reality, thinking that the Bible is only an ideal, a "pie-in-the-sky" that is an idealistic option rather absolute?

In my heart I can imagine what the world would say to Christianity if given the opportunity:

> "Why does the picture we have of the founder of your religion, Jesus Christ, differ so much from what we have seen of you over your history? Why do you hurt each other so badly and why are you so divided? You have so many different names over your doors that we wonder whether or not you are really worshipping and being led by the same God. You are always saying that you are right and others of your same faith are wrong. We often wonder why, if you are reading the same truth, you are so fragmented. Can you not all get together and recognize the fact that your God would want you to be united? Who are we to believe?"
>
> "You seem so unhappy so much of the time. You seem desperate to prove your point and make your case that you don't much seem like Jesus who simply lived and lived simply. You are religious and He wasn't. You have proven to be violent and confrontational and He wasn't. You condemn sin and sinners and He didn't, as a matter of fact we have even been told that

> *He came to cover our sins. He loved but with you it is very difficult to find love – not just love for us but love for each other."*
>
> *"We need to believe in something, in Someone, but why would we believe in your God. If He makes us like He has made you then we don't want Him. If He loves us then you will love us and you will love one another."*
>
> *"We will keep looking and keep making up our own gods because they seem to be better than yours. Come and see us when you get it figured out – if it's not too late."*

The observations in this book are designed to raise questions in the reader's heart. It is hoped that each who pick up this book will realize my desire to see the body of our Lord Jesus Christ, the Church, be all that Jesus died for it to be. It should engender controversy and that is good if it is from different sides desiring the true end.

It would be advisable for the reader to read the appendix, titled **"The Dispensations of Scripture"** first in order to understand the momentous impact of Pentecost and what was ushered in to the faith experience on that day.

Let's look at the facts and explore the problem of the American Church of our day and time.

Chapter 1

Questioning the Church

The church is not just a concept but a reality. She is the Bride of Christ, one day to be presented pure and spotless by the Son to the Father. She was bought and paid for at Calvary and was born at Pentecost, filled with the potential to be Christ on the earth. The Lord gave the church the power to go out in His name and see lives change, lives that would ultimately bring the Father the glory that He is due.

Something happened. The true, blood bought Church has gotten stuck in an antiquated religious system that has robbed her of the power that God intended and that Jesus died for. The world is dying because of the church's ineffectiveness. There are races of people that have never heard the name Jesus and billions of others that have not heard enough about Him to say "yes" or "no" to His offer of redemption. For the most part, it isn't intentional. But things can change. We, the body of Christ can change. We can come out of the broken down system that we find ourselves in.

On January 11, 2002, I presented to the readers of *"Words of Agape"*, our weekday devotional, a question that desperately needed an answer. It asked for reasons that the Church does not show the power that was in the believers of the early Church. If we could determine what is missing in the twenty-first century, we may be able to capture their power, zeal and have similar results.

What Is The Church Supposed To Look Like?

The simplest presentation in Scripture of what the Church should look like is found in *Acts 2:42-47*. We read in *44-47*:

> *"All the believers were **together** and had everything **in common**. Selling their possessions and goods, they gave to anyone as he had need. Every day they continued to meet **together** in the temple courts. They broke bread in their homes and ate **together** with glad and sincere hearts, praising God and enjoying the favor of all the people. And the Lord added to their number daily those who were being saved."* (Emphasis added)

Unity

The words *"together"* and *"everything in common,"* indicate that the people were of the same mind. They had experienced the same thing - salvation and a filling with the Holy Spirit at almost the same time! They were Jews and proselytes and all had sought and accepted the gift of the Holy Spirit on or shortly after Pentecost. Jews from all over the world had made the pilgrimage to Jerusalem for the Feast of Weeks or Pentecost and after this life-changing experience some remained in Jerusalem and many moved in with believers in the city which set up a uniquely intimate lifestyle for everyone. They would have shared their lives and resources, worshipping at different times during the day as people came and went.

Unity is a hallmark of the true Church and there is

nothing inherent that should divide her but much that should unite her. The early Church was together organically not organizationally, meaning that they had a life that was being lived naturally as a result of the Holy Spirit living in them and through them.

Understanding

The Jerusalem Church was going to the Temple (Solomon's Porch) each day probably to hear the teachings of the Twelve, who were telling them about Jesus. They had eaten with Him, slept with Him, talked with Him, lived with Him and were telling the new Christians all about Him and His ways. They were learning the same things with a hunger to know their Lord. They would go back to their homes and celebrate the Lord's Supper which was known then as the *agape* or *love feast* and were coming to understand the magnitude of what had been done on their behalf. There would have been no hierarchy because they all started out together. The teachings of Jesus were so real and their effects were still being experienced by so many of those who had been saved. Remember many of these people had actually seen and heard Jesus themselves.

Fruit

The new believers' ranks were growing. They were rejoicing at the salvation of many new brothers and sisters and the Lord was being praised. There must have been a breathtaking feeling of expectancy every morning at what God was going to do that day and the coming together in the evening for worship must have been a joy. *"And the Lord added to the church daily such as should be saved."* Acts 2:47b

It must have been wonderful for the believers to be

seeing so many powerful things happening. Their focus was always on the power of God rather than their own efforts. They knew that they were seeing God working and not man!

It would seem that the word that best describes the early Church is **family**. They were a family and all of the good things that were to come from the family relationship were happening to them. They were safe, accepted, blessed and were seeing results not from their own efforts but from God's.

What is the Church supposed to look like? It is to look like the most functional and fruitful family that could be imagined. It was a family that was being primed and prepared by God to change the world for millennia to come. That is what we are to look like now!

Take some time to think about all that God could do through us if we were united and understood His plan and His way. The early Church was thrust into a situation that was ripe with potential. God put them in the perfect circumstances to become all that He intended and will do the same for us if we do what they did. Shortly before Jesus' ascension into heaven, He told the disciples, *"Do not leave Jerusalem, but wait for the gift my Father promised which you have heard me speak about. For John baptized with water; but in a few days you will be baptized with the Holy Spirit."* Acts 1:4-5

If we were to put off our religious trappings and truly become a family then we could expect God to do what He did then. Study Church history and see if the Church Jesus died for has ever approached, in one city, what the Jerusalem Church was. In our day there are cities that are nearing this level of Church unity and the power of God is being seen at the levels of Acts. I have heard and read reports from communities around the world of magnificent outpourings of the power of God through Christians being broken and desperate before Him. Revival is possible and I believe with all of my heart that it depends on the accord among the children of God. Unity that results in community transformation is possible! God is waiting for it from His people.

If the Church were one, we would long ago have given every human being the chance to say "yes" or "no" to Christ. We individually reach people and that is good but that is not God's intent. He wants us to cover the earth with His glory, with the power overlapping from one region to another. But what is necessary for this to happen and what must the people of God do to facilitate it?

Chapter 2

Desperation for God

There is a responsibility on each generation of Christians to pass the truth of God to the next generation and a failure to do so is at the heart of the problems in the United States of America. We are a nation blessed beyond measure with our purpose being to share those blessings with the rest of the world. I am not just referring to material blessings but emphasize the fact that our spiritual blessings are unparalleled in human history. Many homes have Bibles in every room, preachers are all over the television and there is a church building in every neighborhood. The freedom to seek Him and proclaim Him is ours but we are still overrun with problems that would seem to say that we have never experienced the goodness of God. Incredible victories in war and in peace belie the fact that God is with us and has a purpose for us. Circumstances in most of the rest of the world should make us realize that it is the American Church that God has a beautiful plan to show Himself to the earth. I am not saying that we are more important than believers anywhere else in the world but we could be special.

The true Church is to be a *"... building fitly framed together (that) growth unto a holy temple in the Lord:*

In whom ye are also builded together for a habitation of God through the Spirit." (Ephesians 2:21-22 KJV)

We are to be a holy temple, a building, a habitation of God through the Spirit! A temple a building, a habitation all have the air of permanence and are expected to last more than one generation. The Church must become the "place" where the Lord truly dwells so that there is no doubt from the world's point of view that we are the people of God.

When I was young boy growing up in Detroit, Michigan in the 1950's and 60's, our neighborhood was primarily Polish and Italian with a few other nationalities sprinkled in. Catholicism was the main religious tradition and the churches were full on Sunday mornings. I was a Catholic and our church had five masses (services) with the 10:30am, 11:45am and 1:00pm services full most of the time. Most of the neighborhood was religious.

Can you remember back to a time when air conditioning was not common like it is today? It made for some very interesting summer nights. Our windows and most other homes left their windows open at night and much of what was going on in the other houses could be heard very clearly. I heard the turmoil in the lives of my neighbors and they heard what was going on in our house and through it all I wondered where the God that we worshipped on Sunday was during the rest of the week. How could peoples' faith have absolutely no effect on their everyday lives? It couldn't be real!

Life was difficult with severe asthma and there was little peace in our family? Where was God? My mother, aunt and grandmother would have masses said for me, relatives sent holy water from Lourdes, in France, to anoint me with but nothing ever changed. My young and searching heart didn't understand what good church did for people. As soon as I could get out, I would.

Even though I felt the need for God and truth in my heart the only place I felt I could turn was to the wisdom of men.

Broken Cisterns

In my adolescence and young adult years I searched the writings of anyone that I thought might have the answer – nothing was real, nothing made sense. There were too many loose ends and those that I hoped had the answer were simply putting the question in different ways. I wound up feeling worse because of the frustration of those whose writings I read or who I read about. Vincent Van Gogh, a tragic man who seemed to be looking for love and acceptance, never found it. His misery showed through even in the bright paintings that showed beauty and color to everyone but himself. The eastern mystics or those who wrote about them fascinated me but I could see that the key in that philosophy was to look inside oneself and come to perfection and realization there. Inside of me was nothing of truth or value. How could God be involved in the lives of man who was responsible for such evil on the earth? Tragedy seemed to stalk so many of those that had a hunger to know. Instead of being answered, the questions just piled higher and higher and frustration and despondency set in. I took on an "eat, drink, and be merry for tomorrow we die" attitude.

A life that was spiraling out of control continued even with a wonderful wife and precious little son. A day in February, 1978 was marked by a phone call from my wife from her mother's house telling me that she wouldn't be coming home, that she needed to be apart from me for a while finding it impossible to live with my despair. I was crushed and brought to the point of giving up. Drinking and marijuana became my escape but it took far too much to get me out of the hurt that I was feeling.

One day a friend of mine and I bought a case of beer and had a bag of pot and we proceeded to consume most of it. Nothing took the pain away! When my friend left, I realized just how miserable I was. I stood in the bedroom with tears streaming down my face. Something inside of me told me to cry out. I cried, "Oh God, please help me. Please!"

Immediately the phone rang and it was the girl next door whose husband had been giving me little bits and pieces of truth over the past few months. She said, "Are you through getting drunk yet?" I said "yes" and knew in my heart that this was the beginning of God's answer to my cry. He had heard me! I needed to be desperate. In order to understand what He was going to teach me, I had to be desperate. Desperate! My neighbor told me to take a nap and get cleaned up and come over. We would have pizza and they would talk to me. I rested calm and peaceful because I knew that the answers were there.

Later that evening I heard wonderful truths that changed me, transformed me from being dead in trespasses and sins to being alive in Christ. They told me that I had an enemy but because of the sacrifice of Jesus I was victorious over him. I felt alive, I felt free!

Don't get me wrong. There were other Christians that witnessed to me. Pastors would come from area churches to the house to talk to me (I think I might have been a "trophy"). I was always polite to them and as they were getting ready to leave they would ask me to kneel down. They would ask me to repeat the words that they prayed from my heart. I would say their words out loud after them and they would praise the Lord and pat me on the back inviting me to church. I would tell them that I would try to get there and they would leave. For all of their good hearted care for me I would get up off my knees just as dead in trespasses and sins as I was before they came, before I knelt and before they invited me to church. I didn't see anything! When they visited I saw that they cared but there were no answers. Only in the display of power, the phone ringing at my cry, did I see something. How did my neighbors know when to call? How could it have been right when I cried? There was power there. What all of the men and women that I had read were looking for was answered in being desperate before God and crying to Him. Being helpless and knowing it was what it was about. Knowing that a human being is incapable of saving themselves is the knowledge that frees, liberates and opens prison doors.

People are searching. I talk to them often about their desire for God but then their distrust and sometimes even disgust for the church surfaces. Their disgust is at what we have labeled church and not at the true blood bought, redeemed Church, the body of Our Lord and Savior Jesus Christ. You see, they just haven't been exposed to the true Church enough to have been effected by it. They are looking at those who call themselves Christians to be the true Church. They need to make a proper informed choice of whether to accept the sacrifice of Christ based on a true representation of Him on the earth. I didn't know it but that is what I was looking for. Something real! Something powerful and life changing!

We must become the living, breathing body of Christ and we must be interracial, intergenerational and international. We must cover the earth. The influence of Christ must not be subject to all the things that have historically divided the people of God and brought us together in segregated clusters.

The people of America are looking for true spiritual power. They summon psychics; they are fascinated by the occult. Harry Potter and anything else that intimates that there is something supernatural even if it can't be trusted is popular.

Americans worry about the future and the response of the Church is that America must turn from her wicked ways. We've missed it! It is not America but the Church in America that must repent.

II Chronicles 7:13-14 says. *"When I shut up the heavens so that there is no rain, or command locusts to devour the land or send a plague among my people, if my people who are called by my name, will humble themselves and pray and seek my face and turn from their wicked ways, then will I hear from heaven and will forgive their sin and will heal their land."* God is coming to His people, not the unbelieving world, about the issue of repentance.

> *I Peter 4:17,*
> *"For it is time for judgment to begin with the family of God; and if it begins with us, what will the outcome be for those who do not obey the gospel of God?"*

The context of *I Peter 4* is believers in Christ being judged by God for their effect on the world. Verse *19* says *"So then, those who suffer according to God's will should commit themselves to their faithful Creator and continue to do good."* We commit our souls, our lives to Him *"to do good"*, in Greek *"agathopolia"*, which means *virtue*. Our characteristics in the world's eyes should be a people who are involved in a virtuous life style, in changing the world for the better. If we take the rest of the fourth chapter of *I Peter* in its context, and finish the thoughts of verses *12-19*, then we will see that the tendency of the Church is to get away from the qualities that will communicate the reality of Christ to the world.

It is the responsibility of those entrusted with the oversight of the body to communicate God's heart to the people. The leadership of the Church, the elders, are told in *5:2-3* to, *"Be shepherds of God's flock that is under your care, serving as overseers – not because you must, but because you are willing, as God wants you to be; not greedy for money, but eager to serve; not lording it over those entrusted to you, but being examples to the flock."*

Has the leadership of the Church exhibited the qualities of oversight or protective covering over the body? Yes, at times, but has it been the character of church leadership consistently and would the world make that judgment of us? If we are to show the righteousness of God to a lost world and their opinion is that we haven't, then are we in need of repentance?

If the answer to any of the questions that have been raised are not what God would expect then we are in need of change.

The world is in desperate need of Christ but does not know it. We must show them.

Chapter 3

Looking For the Power of God

My answer from God came as the result of a cry from deep inside and God responded with a show of power and concern. The cry came from years of frustration and from desperation and hopelessness and led to a discovery of truth. I had always wanted to believe in something or someone outside of myself, a source of knowledge that would forever end the idea of, "I think."

I had never read a Bible, our family didn't own one. As a boy I was told that only a priest could ascertain what God meant and there was no need for the common person to read Scripture. This later led me to the probability that much of what I had been taught all those years might not be true. This was easy to accept because I had never seen any changed lives in the people who taught and believed what I had been taught. The sickness, fighting, divorce, drinking and frustration with life that I saw in "Christians" when compared to those who were simply living their lives outside of church showed very little difference. Aren't unregenerate human beings only influenced by what they can see, hear, feel, taste and smell? There was no other way for me to make decisions other than by what my senses showed me and what I didn't realize and what those who are lost at this moment do not realize is that God is pursuing them. He is arranging the things in their lives, through the work of the Holy Spirit, to bring them to the point of faith. This is where the Church comes in. **His desire is that we would be the people that show the world sensually what God does spiritually.**

Truth came into my life and will come into every life that truly wants it. For me, God said, "Now you are ready!" In my desperation God said, "Now you can understand that I am everything because you are nothing. Now I can make you something." He showed me.

After my new birth experience, my Bible study increased and my thinking graduated from what I should be to what the church should be. In looking at the first century church and the church of today, confusion crept back into my heart. When I read Acts and saw the power of the proclaimed Word to save people AND deliver them, I again had the feeling that something was wrong. The crippled man in Acts 3 had been laid daily at the temple gate Beautiful and was healed as Peter and John held out their hands and spoke inspired words. The sick of Jerusalem were laid in the streets so that Peter's shadow might fall on them for healing (*Acts 5:15-16*) and there are many more examples. Why were the apostles and the Church of Acts walking in this power and not the church of today? Was God not the same God with the same purpose – to redeem mankind? I wondered what we were doing different or not doing at all. Did our faith get corrupted and if so, how could we reverse it?

God began, gradually, to answer some of these questions, a little bit at a time, as I was able to grasp and understand. He even gave me some personal displays of His power.

Helpless by Ben's Bed

A couple of months after I was made pastor of a small Baptist church, I was asked by one of our members to visit her father who was in the hospital waiting for open heart surgery. I went the next day and was very much taken by the man, Ben. We talked for quite a while about everything from baseball to Rush Limbaugh but never got around to talking about Jesus which when I realized this, on the way home, I became very upset. How could I allow an opportunity to witness to a non-Christian go by without introducing him to the Lord? The next day he was having the surgery so my opportunity was probably gone until after he was well. I spent the day with his family while the operation was going on and after it was over the Doctor asked us all to come back in the unit to talk to us. He said that Ben had done just fine and we could see him the next day. I then said a prayer of thanksgiving and they were all very pleased and blessed.

The next day I visited Ben again and was amazed at how good he looked. We talked about the fact that he had a loving and supportive family and how happy he was. When it was time to leave, I told him that I would be leaving town for the next few days but would be back to see him then. He said that I would have to come and visit him at home because he would not still be there and this, again, was fine with me. On the way home I realized that I had not presented Christ to him again and was extremely disappointed with myself and wondered why I would fail to do something so important. It was out of character. I made up my mind that as soon as I returned from my trip I would present him with the gospel.

The next Monday night when I returned home, I called his daughter and asked how he was doing. She said that he had had a massive heart attack and the family would have to decide soon about keeping him on life support. I told her that I would be there first thing in the morning and please don't do anything yet.

When I entered the cardiac ICU and saw him lying in bed, I was almost sick to my stomach. How could I have been so incompetent? He had tubes all over and a respirator was breathing for him and he had the most pained look on his face that I had ever seen. I stood next to his bed in total disgust with myself and with circumstances. How could I have missed the opportunities to tell him about Jesus? At that moment, I pointed my nose to the sky and said out loud, "What am I here for now Lord? What do you want me to do now? Forgive me Lord, I blew it!" I felt an urge to pray a prayer that was not my own. I prayed for maybe ten minutes. I prayed that because God had a captive audience, would He please just speak to Ben. "Don't let him go anywhere until you've convinced him of your love and your forgiveness, Lord." "Keep him where he is until you've convinced him of what Christ did for him." I also prayed that he would recover physically.

As I prayed an incredible thing began to happen. His right hand, which I had been holding in my right hand, at his side, began to move. It slowly moved up over his stomach heading to his chest. When it got over his heart, it stopped and his hand fell back to his side while my hand stayed over his heart. I finished my prayer and left wondering what had happened and prayed that God would work a miracle in Ben's life.

God was orchestrating the circumstances to show His power and my dependence on His power. Only God could put everything together, set everything up to show that He is God and has not changed from the time I have read about in the book of Acts.

The next morning when I called to find out how he was doing, I was told that he had come out of the coma and was recovering well. I raced to the hospital to see him and was shocked to find him sitting up in bed. This was something I had not expected even though I believed God. As we talked, I told him of the details of my prayer of the day before and told him about his hand moving my hand and asked him what that was and asked what he was trying to tell me. He said that he did not remember any of that but that he wanted me to know that he had given his heart to Jesus Christ! Joy and praise welled up inside of me as I knew that I had learned a very valuable lesson: **God was still willing to do mighty works to show Himself to His people and the world but these works would need to come out of our helplessness, brokenness and dependence. <u>He will need to receive all of the glory.</u> <u>He must increase and we must decrease.</u> Our agendas and talents and self sufficiency must become broken and the character of the early Church must become our character.** They waited, simply waited for His power to arrive. It has.

Over the years since Ben's healing, I have seen God do so many things to bring glory to Himself. He has constantly shown His love for His people and His desire to use us in His work of redemption on the earth.

When I watch the well known preachers and teachers on television or in person or hear them on the radio, I used to compare myself to them. Almost every one of them has more hair than I do, there are few that weigh as much as I do and most of them have a southern twang. I don't. I have a course Yankee accent accompanied by arms flying everywhere. God wants to work in the trenches with the common people, called by His name, in everyday life. He wants to work through people who say, "What do I do now?" He wants to perform mighty works through common people in fellowship with Himself and with each other. He doesn't want the healing done by a blue haired man on a stage in Jacksonville or Los Angeles but by believers on streets and in homes, ministering the love of Christ to those who have the needs. He wants the deliverance to come out of fellowship – communion with Him and one another.

The Last Days

In *2 Timothy 3:2-4* Paul tells young Timothy some of the characteristics of people in the last days." He says that they will be lovers of themselves and that in being lovers of themselves they will be *"... lovers of money, boastful, proud, abusive, disobedient to their parents, ungrateful, unholy, without love, unforgiving, slanderous, without self control, brutal, not lovers of the good, treacherous, rash, conceited, lovers of pleasure rather than lovers of God – having a form of godliness but denying its power. Have nothing to do with them"*. One of the traits of the time in which we live will be that people (even Christians) will deny the power of God.

What needs to be guarded against and challenged is that the faithful remnant are so many generations removed from the power of God being seen and expected that we have even been convinced that things are different now than they were in the first century. I am sure in my heart that there is a profound but very simple reason for this – **Broken Cisterns.**

Chapter 4

"Forsaking Niagara"

Think about the power of Niagara Falls. If you have never been there or seen pictures I can attest to the fact that it is one of the most awesome, powerful sights that you will ever see. 194,940 gallons of water fall over the cliff every second! The rocks at the bottom have been pounded by that water for millennia and man has been tapping its resources for centuries. It has produced hydroelectric power, and has overall just been a wonderful spectacle as long as man has lived on this continent.

I remember going to the Falls in Ontario, Canada when I was a child because my mother grew up in nearby Hamilton. I would stand by the railing and watch the falls crash to the canyon floor. The mist would rise and on a sunny day there was a perpetual rainbow as the miniscule water droplets would break the sunlight into all the colors of the spectrum. Even from blocks away at the hotel you could hear the thunder of the water and feel the dampness even on a warm summer day. I would wonder where all that water was coming from and where it was going.

Now think what it would be like for someone to take some of the water of Niagara, put it in a bucket and then insinuate that it was the same thing and that the water in the bucket was doing the same thing as the water going over the falls. This is absurd yet this would be a fitting parallel to the actions of the children of Israel in the Old Testament book of Jeremiah. They were forsaking the powerful, immeasurable Jehovah and taking little bits of His character, combining His power with the "power" of other gods and calling it their faith and belief.

> *"My people have committed two sins; they have forsaken me, the fountain of living water, and have dug their own cisterns, broken cisterns that can hold no water."*
> Jeremiah 2:13

Sin Number One

God says that His people, Israel, had committed two sins: First, they had forsaken Him who is a fountain, a never ending source of power, refreshment, awe, inspiration and direction. They determined that they would turn their back on this incredible source and instead take little bits back to where they felt safe and could be in complete control. This is man's nature. He must be able to determine a plan beforehand because anything outside of what he controls, he fears, and what he fears, he rejects. This is acceptable if what he rejects only affects him and his efforts but in saying "no" to God, he comes in the way of God being glorified on the earth. Because of this, the forsaking of the source of perfect power, the nations are dying and going to hell!

In the book of Acts, there is a beautiful progression in the development of the Church. We hear Jesus tell His disciples to *"... tarry at Jerusalem for the promise of the Father."* He is telling them to wait for the coming of the power of the Holy Spirit. This power would change the world if allowed because it is an inherent power, a power that must be activated. It is in the Church but must be lived, let loose, like dynamite must be lit. The word for this power in the Greek is *dunamis* and is actually the word from which we derive the word dynamite. There is awesome potential in one of those sticks but it must be activated and the Church for many centuries has decided not to fire it up.

> *"But you will receive power* ("dunamis"*) when the Holy Spirit comes upon you..."*
> Acts 1:8

Simply basking under the *"fountain of living waters"* will unleash this power just like on Pentecost. The disciples were in worship of God, waiting; expecting that what Jesus said would come would truly come. They were where they were supposed to be, doing what they were supposed to be doing, worshipping and waiting. When this awesome promise came, they were changed and so was the world around them. Three thousand were saved the first day, not through the impetus of the disciples but by the power of God! Then believers were added, then multiplied, churches were added then churches multiplied, there was peace, the Lord's hand was with them and the Word continued to increase and finally, *"...the churches were strengthened in the faith and grew daily in numbers." Acts 16:5*

It was overwhelming what God was doing! There wasn't any time for programs or plans because the Church was being washed and energized by the "fountain of living waters." They didn't have time to do anything but watch God work.

Peter and John were walking into the Temple (*Acts 3:1-10*), and walked past a man who was begging. Peter stopped dead in his tracks and said, *"Silver and gold have I none but such as I have I give you. In the name of*

Jesus of Nazareth, rise up and walk." When you are standing under the spring, the fountain, you will not need to sit down and decide what you should do next. You will be about the business of your life, waiting eagerly for God to do what He's going to do next.

Picture the Church walking in revelation and inspiration. Things were happening because the Holy Spirit was in control. The purposes of the Father were being lived by the believers and things were being accomplished. The Church had favor with God and the secular world.

What we see in Acts is "Abel religion" - true spirituality. E. W. Bullinger wrote in his work **"Rightly Dividing The Word Of Truth"**; *"God has given us a way of righteousness but man has invented a way of his own and those two ways are brought before us upon the very fore front of Revelation, the way of God and the way of man – the one which Abel took and the other that Cain invented. These are the only two ways from that moment to this."* This should scare the daylights out of the Church! Have we chosen the way of Cain, the way that leads to death without even knowing it? If, like Bullinger says, there are only two ways, the way of Abel and the way of Cain, then we are forced to examine what we are in light of the conviction of the Word. Have we chosen the broken cistern? If so, how could we? What would possess us to give up this freedom, this expectancy, and this power? God explains what happened to His people when He puts forth the second sin.

Sin Number Two

Simply put, we have built something to take His place. Not only did we turn from the fountain but we have built something to take the fountains' place! Israel did it, the Church did it! These are our religious systems and when compared to His glory they should be seen for what they really are – nothing. They can hold no water and what doesn't manage to leak out or dry up, stagnates. We look to our own works and programs, our own ideas and say that we have Him. We replace relationship and obedience with good works. We set up a sacrificial system of our own, not God's and proceed to make ourselves feel good because of what we do rather than what we are. He chastises us for it but as usual continues to extend the invitation of relationship and love and deals with us in that love. He simply wants us to realize that we are pitiful in our efforts.

A cistern is a large vessel that collects rain and groundwater and holds it in store for use later. It has always been a common way for people to ensure that they will have water during dry times. To dig one takes some time especially if it is being hewn out of solid rock. The religious systems, cisterns, that we have built, have taken centuries, even millennia to build. It must not take that long to tear down. It must happen now and by those who realize what has taken place and there must be a sense of urgency. We must be rid of these monstrosities. Whatever has kept Him from being glorified by His people must go no matter what the cost.

Complicated, expensive, conglomerates have replaced the simple ways that God moved the truth of Jesus and His salvation over the world two thousand years ago. We have replaced organic unity with organizational structure and hierarchy and taken the beauty of people dwelling in oneness and instead promoted fragmented and isolated programs.

We have rejected the gifts of God to those in the Church in favor of paid ministers who are not gifted in so many of the functions they, by necessity, must perform. In the early Church, if there was the need for a prophet or if the Church needed evangelists, He raised them up. He was in control and His people knew nothing other than to let Him. We will deal with these issues later in more detail.

Our goal should not be to "hold water" as our text

insinuates but is to give the power of the river a course to follow. The river uses the path of least resistance to flow to the sea and it must flow there because that is its purpose. It empties into the great oceans and evaporates and falls again to nourish the earth. God must not find us guilty of damming His rivers and diverting His purposes. He is the one who flows, He is the great fountain and we must be the path of least resistance. Our religious "mountains and dams" need to be leveled off, torn down and we must be the soft stone that He flows through, changed by Him, shaped by Him. As He flows over us and through us, the world must get their refreshment and power through us.

In 1997 I took a mission trip to Russia and Belarus. I was extremely fascinated with Russia, especially the Kremlin. On one side of Red Square is a marble building called Lenin's Tomb and holds the remains of the father of Russian communism, Vladimir Lenin. As the line winds through the building on the way to the glass enclosed pier, there is a reverent air about the people because for communists everywhere, he was a pioneer. When you get to his stand, there he looks like he just decided to lie down and take a nap. It is amazing how lifelike he looks. The fact remains though, he is dead. Even though he appears to be alive and people speak about him like that body is really him, he is gone; it is just a shell. I shudder to say what I am now going to say but the church as we now know it may look alive but is just the shell of what Christ envisioned when He said, *"But you will receive power when the Holy Spirit comes on you: and you shall be my witnesses in Jerusalem, and in all Judea and Samaria, and to the ends of the earth." Acts 1:8*

The world looks at Christianity and snickers. Leo Tolstoy said that *"The only thing wrong with Christianity is that nobody has ever tried it."* When we are given the arguments against our faith we are told how Christianity has been responsible for so much of the pain of history. Many of the trouble spots in the world today involve religion and often Christianity. What is being talked about is not true, fundamental, rudimentary Christianity though. People living in fellowship with God and each other, *"esteeming each other better than ourselves," (Philippians 2:3) and "submit to one another out of reverence for Christ," (Ephesians 5:21)* is what Christianity is all about. Being willing to die for each other as Christ died for us is to be the hallmark of our faith. I am here to say "thus saith the Lord" and proclaim that we must "try it." We are compelled by the Word of God to become, individually and corporately, what the Word says we are to be

What we have built will not hold water. The religious systems of the earth do nothing more than allow us to shape Him, make Him into our own image and likeness. They are nothing more than containers for our idols; pockets to keep them in. These systems actually mask the need to be the true Church. We make excuses for what we have done saying that over the centuries many who know much about God have said "this or that" but nothing changes what God says:

"... they have hewn themselves cisterns, broken cisterns that can hold no water."

Chapter 5

The People of God

The book of Jeremiah was written at a time in Israel's history between the fall of the northern kingdom of Israel and the southern kingdom of Judah. After the death of Solomon, a conflict between the rightful heir to the throne, Rehoboam and a labor leader under Solomon, Jeroboam, resulted in the United Kingdom being torn into two separate and distinct nations. Jeremiah was speaking to the southern nation of Judah which consisted of the two tribes of Benjamin and Judah. At the time of Jeremiah, the northern kingdom, Israel, had already fallen to the Assyrians and Judah was being warned of the possibility of the same fate. He spoke to Judah in the time leading up to its fall and the demise of its capitol, Jerusalem, by the Babylonians. The defeat of Israel preceded Judah's by one hundred thirty six years. As a kingdom, they had a succession of bad kings punctuated by a good one here and there. They had experienced a revival of sorts under one of those godly kings, Josiah, who brought the Word of God back into the life of the nation and broad reforms instituted by him led the people to a heart of repentance. This repentance was absolutely necessary to head off God's judgment upon the land.

It needed to be long lived and to be deep and generational and it needed to be a renewal that changed forever the way these people looked at their relationship with God from a national perspective.

At this time in their history, Jeremiah prophesied to Judah her ultimate fall unless certain conditions were met. He speaks the word of God powerfully and eloquently in our text, *Jeremiah 2:13*.

> *"For my people have committed two evils: they have forsaken me, the fountain of living waters, and hewn them out cisterns, broken cisterns, that can hold no water."*
>
> *(KJV)*

God is talking to His people – the people of His name. He is talking to the ones whom He brought miraculously out of Egypt and sent into the world. He is addressing those whom He has formed to announce His glory to the earth – *"My people"*!

God is talking to His people and the very first area in which Israel forsook Him was in being His people. They rejected Him and took other gods as their own. Most of the time they still considered Him the God of their past but as for their present there were other gods, gods that could bring them fertility and production in other areas of life. Molech, Baal, Ashtar were some that they went whoring after. These were the gods of other peoples. Each nation had a god of their own invention and when humans formulate something it will usually be something that brings them pleasure. The gods of other lands usually had sex as their main act of worship. Temple prostitutes both male and female were supposed to represent the fertility which was so important to the peoples that derived their livelihood from the soil. Israel's allegiance had been divided for a long time but throughout scripture,

God is always extending His hand of forgiveness and reconciliation. That's what Jeremiah 2:13 is all about.

In our verse, God says that He is addressing His people – the people of His name. He is talking to those that He delivered out of Egypt, led in the wilderness and delivered into the Promised Land. God established them in a land that was flowing with milk and honey. If the first five books of the Bible, the Pentateuch, written by Moses, are looked at as a unit, it will be seen that God is showcasing His children for the entire world to see. Was the pillar of cloud by day and the pillar of fire by night just for Israel or could everyone who lived in the land see them?

God had His people in the land avenue of the Middle Eastern world between Egypt and Mesopotamia and they would have contact with all the major cultures of the ancient world. Jehovah was showing what could be accomplished by a nation that He was dedicated to and who remained dedicated to Him.

Israel Is the Prototype

From the fall of man, God has sought to build a people to communicate Himself to the world. With Abraham, God pulled a family out of all the earth and built a nation that He would establish forever. He said to him,

> *"And in thy seed all the nations of the earth shall be blessed;"*

He built them up numerically during the captivity in Egypt where they went from a family of seventy to a nation of up to two million and came out of that slavery with a national identity. He also gave them land, a geographical home with a deed granted by Jehovah to the land of promise. Here is the deed:

"Command the sons of Israel and say to them, 'When you enter the land of Canaan, this is the land that shall fall to you as an inheritance, even the land of Canaan according to its borders. Your southern sector shall extend from the wilderness of Zin along the side of Edom, and your southern border shall extend from the end of the Salt Sea eastward. Then your border shall turn direction from the south to the ascent of Akrabbim, and continue to Zin, and its termination shall be to the south of Kadesh-Barnea; and it shall reach Hazareddar, and continue to Azmon. And the border shall turn direction from Azmon to the brook of Egypt, and its termination shall be at the sea. As for the western border, you shall have the Great Sea, that is its coastline this shall be your western border. And this shall be your north border: from the Great Sea ye shall point out for you Mt.Hor: From Mt.Hor ye shall point out your border unto the entrance of Hamath; and the goings forth of the border shall be to Zedad: and the border shall go on to Ziphron, and the goings out of it shall be at Hazar-enan: this shall be your north border. And ye shall point out your east border from Hazar-enan to Shepham: And the coast shall go down from Shapham to Riblah, on the east side of Ain; and the border shall descend, and shall reach unto the side of the sea of Chinnereth eastward: And the border shall go down to Jordan, and the goings out of it shall be at the salt sea: this shall be your land with the coasts thereof."
Numbers 34:1-12 (KJV)

Again let me emphasize that God was establishing a land for His **people**. Through a nation dealing with other nations God chose to show Himself. This is such an integral principle throughout the Old Testament. In *Numbers 14*, Moses is in a dialogue with God concerning the unfaithfulness of Israel. They were grumbling, whimpering, weeping and wanting to go back to Egypt. God said:

> *"How long will this people spurn me? And how long will they not believe in me, despite all the signs which I have performed in their midst? I will smite them with pestilence and dispossess them, and I will make you into a nation greater and mightier than they."*
>
> *"But Moses said to the Lord, "Then the Egyptians will hear of it, for by thy strength Thou didst bring up this people from their midst, and they will tell it to the inhabitants of this land. They have heard that Thou O Lord, art in the midst of this people, for Thou, O Lord, art seen eye to eye, while Thy cloud stands over them; and Thou dost go before them in a pillar of cloud by day and in a pillar of fire by night."*

"Now if Thou dost slay this people as one man, then the nations who have heard of Thy fame will say, "Because the Lord could not bring this people into the land which He promised them by oath, therefore He slaughtered them in the wilderness." But now I pray, let the power of the Lord be great, just as Thou hast declared..."

Numbers 14:13-17 (KJV)

Everything about Israel's reaction to His power was a direct reflection on God to the nations who had contact with them. In other words, "the whole world was watching." God chooses human beings put together in community to communicate His glory.

In building Israel, God did not leave any area of their life without guidance and direction. He declared and established the law for them, He elaborated all that they should and should not do. Nutritional laws, social laws, religious guidelines, rules about dealing with foreigners were all meant to show God's people as holy before all the other nations. If obeyed, these directives would produce a separate and holy people.

Think about all the peoples in the land of Canaan that were seeing Israel with a pillar of cloud by day and a pillar of fire by night going with them wherever they went. They all had heard about the fact that God had actually parted the sea in order for the Hebrews to pass through while Pharaoh's army was swallowed up by the crashing walls of water. They surely had found out that the ramparts of Jericho had fallen, not by battering rams or sledges but by faith that resulted in trumpet blasts. What must they have thought? Their gods were not capable of anything like this! Their gods were inanimate – dumb. Only Israel had a God who actually was making them into something for His own names' sake. What other people saw in the Israelites they attributed to God; both good and bad.

The Hebrews were a people called by God to proclaim His glory to the nations! That was their purpose and that was their mandate. What they actually did though was turn their backs on His ways and His Word. What they did was forsake the fountain of living waters."

The Church Is Now the People Called By His Name

We have already established that God has determined to use people brought together in community to communicate His qualities to the unbelieving world. In the year 606 BC the southern kingdom of Judah experienced the final defeat of the nation with its capitol, Jerusalem, falling twenty years later in 586 BC. This spelled the end of the nation of Israel as it had been known for centuries because the Temple was destroyed, the priesthood was liquidated and the sacrificial system was left without a venue in which to be carried out. A smaller Temple was rebuilt by the exiles sent back with Zerubbabel and Ezra and Israelite worship began again but was sporadic from that time forward because of invasions and occupations by the Greeks and Romans. The New Testament Temple, built by Herod was completely destroyed as Jesus had prophesied in *Matthew 24:1-2*

> *"And Jesus went out, and departed from the temple: and his disciples came to him for to show him the buildings of the temple. And Jesus said unto them, See ye not all these things? Verily I say unto you, there shall not be left one stone upon another, that shall not be thrown down."*
> *(KJV)*

In 70AD, the Roman Titus and his troops, came in and sacked and destroyed the city, dispersing the Jews over the known world. The Jews as the people of God, the nation of God, have never been salt and light since the death of Solomon and are in a state of rejection of the "kingship" of Christ. They will become what God intended at a later time but for now God is using them in their unbelief. Great scientific minds, musical geniuses, financial giants and powers in all other human endeavors are filled with the names of Jews.

They have influenced the world but not for the Messiah. For now there is another people and nation that fills in the gap – the Church.

The blood bought, redeemed Church is not found in the prophesies of the Old Testament. All of the scriptures before Christ are written to Israel and even the promises to them that pertain to the future are written specifically to them. For instance, the prophecy of the "new covenant" in Jeremiah 31, *"This is the covenant I will make **with the house of Israel** after that time," declares the Lord." Jer.31:33a* He is talking about a time in the future when He will restore Israel to nationhood in the land. This is in the process of happening but is not yet complete and the hearts of the people have not changed. There are many other prophecies that are still future regarding Israel. God speaks of the Temple being rebuilt and about the priesthood and sacrificial system being re-instituted.

There is a new covenant given to Jew and Gentile alike and it is effect right now. If you are a believer in Christ then you live under this covenant. It is stated in *Romans 10:9&10, "That if you confess with your mouth, "Jesus is Lord," and believe in your heart that God has raised Him from the dead, you will be saved. For it is with your heart that you believe and are justified, and it is with your mouth that you confess and are saved."*

God says that if we will believe and confess then He will save us. This is a covenant, an agreement between two parties that binds them to permanent relationship with individual and shared responsibilities. We are a covenant people just like the Jews! The Church of Jesus Christ is the people of God in the world today. We do not supplant Israel but we are in covenant in a different dispensation. **(Appendix – "The Dispensations of Scripture")** We will one day be raptured from this earth and Israel will once again be the vehicle of the message of salvation with all of their religious life restored. They will again be the nation that shows the glory of the Lord because they will accept the Messiah, Jesus Christ.

What Is His Intention For The Church?

> *"But because of His great love for us, God, who is rich in mercy, made us alive with Christ even when we were dead in transgressions – it is by grace you have been saved. And God raised us up with Christ and seated us with him in the heavenly realms in Christ Jesus,* **in order that in the coming ages he might show the incomparable riches of his grace, expressed in his kindness to us in Christ Jesus."**
>
> Ephesians 2:4-7

We are saved so that in the coming ages (*aion, dispensations*) *"he might show the incomparable riches of his grace, expressed in his kindness to us in Christ Jesus."* Who does he want to show his riches and grace to? Us, certainly, but also to those with whom we share this planet! He wants the earth to know the extent of His grace and kindness as they watch how He deals with the Church. They can only see the victories that God gives if they see Him give them to the Church and the Church give Him the honor and the praise for them. They can only know deliverance when they see those who are His delivered.

When it becomes obvious in *Acts 10* that God is extending his offer of salvation and relationship outside the confines of Judaism, to a Roman, Cornelius and his family, Peter says, *"I now realize how true it is that God does not show favoritism but accepts men from every nation who fear him and do what is right. You know the message God sent to the people of Israel, telling them the good news of peace through Jesus Christ who is Lord of all." Verses 34-36*

God doesn't merely accept men of all nations, He actually pursues them. He is Lord of all! He sent the message of peace through Jesus Christ to Israel and wants the same message heard by the entire world for He is Lord of all!

If one will simply read the Word of God, reading what is written, putting everything out of their mind concerning preconceived notions of how God wants to do things, the Truth becomes very simple. The Church is to be a united people, one in Christ, totally one in purpose, just as the Father and the Son are. The nations or *ethnos(gr)*, the families of the earth are to hear what God is capable of doing through us for the simple purpose of bringing praise to His name. Inherent in the body of Christ is power, resurrection power, given by Jesus Christ to his disciples on the hillside in Galilee. He said: *"All authority in heaven and earth has been given unto me. Therefore, go and make disciples of all nations, baptizing them in the name of the Father and of the Son and of the Holy Spirit, and teaching them to obey everything I have commanded you. And surely I am with you even to the end of the age." Matthew 28:18-20* Yes, He is speaking to the twelve but He also says that He would be with them until the end of the age and I know that has not yet come and the twelve are not still alive. It was an authority that would be passed down to all who would ever believe. He also told them in *Acts 1:8, "But you shall receive power when the Holy Spirit comes upon you; and you will be my witnesses in Jerusalem, and in all Judea, and Samaria and to the ends of the earth."* If we were to believe that the power was only given to the twelve then it would be safe to assume that the "Great Commission" (*Matthew 28:16-20*) was only given to the twelve.

There is a power that is supposed to accompany the proclamation of the gospel. *Romans 1:16* reads, *"I am not ashamed of the gospel, because it is the power of God for the salvation of everyone who believes: first for the Jew, then for the Gentile."* The gospel has a power attached to it that saves and changes lives. It does things in people because the One that it proclaims did things for people!

If we deny the power, if we walk in a benign set of rules and regulations, the world will never be changed. What we have done is *"forsake (Him) the fountain of living waters and hewn themselves cisterns broken cisterns that can hold no water."* Mankind is crawling around looking for someone's garment to touch like the woman with issue of blood (*Mark 5:25-34*). People are spending all their resources on getting "healed" the world's way when we have been introduced to the "fountain of living waters" and must introduce Him to them.

Why do you think that Paul calls the Church the "body of Christ"? Is it simply a figure of speech or a casual metaphor? It is truth. The Church is to be Him on the earth! We are to minister as He did, to the same kinds of people that He did, doing the same kinds of things in the same kinds of places.

> *"I tell you the truth, anyone who has faith in me will do what I have been doing. He will do even greater things than these because I am going to the Father."*
>
> *(John 14:12)*

Picture the Church covering this earth in the same power and presence as Jesus did two thousand years ago. Think of us ministering in His name doing the same things that He did but on an even bigger scale. We walk down a street and find someone who is sick. We cup their face in our hands and ask if they would like to be healed. They say "yes" and all the believers present begin to pray and speak words of inspiration, with authority into the person's life. They receive and are healed. This is the way it should work. In a service, rather than a man standing up front, the body of Christ gathers around the sick or oppressed person and prays the power of God into their situation. It would be OK because Jesus authorized it when He said, *"But ye shall receive power, after the Holy Ghost is come upon you; and ye shall be my witnesses... "* The Church receives the power from Him and operates in it in the world.

Did Jesus walk down one street with one doctrine and down another street with another doctrine? Surely He was consistent and sure in the truth that He lived and spoke. Not so now! We are not one. The body of Christ is a misnomer because "body" means an organic unity in one flesh; from its most simple cellular form to the most complex of all life. A living thing must operate in unity or it defies its nature. When the Church forsakes the fountain of living waters and makes broken cisterns that can hold no water, it is going against its nature and no good can result.

When Jesus told His disciples in *John 14:12* that those who have faith in Him will do the things that He did and even greater things than He did, He meant it - but we deny it. We have explained them away and instead made up a religious system that has denied and replaced the power of God in ministry. Our system has left the world that should have had ample opportunity to hear of Him, die and go to hell. God help us because it is not too late. There is still time to go back and get rid of what has confined us. We can still become the "People of God."

Chapter 6

The Same Heart and Love

A statement that most would have a hard time arguing with is that the Church is divided. The reasons for the division are varied and diverse and it also must be understood that all division is not inherently wrong.

God had separated the children of Israel into tribes with different inheritances of land in diverse parts of the geography. They had different personalities and characteristics, different strengths and weaknesses and were designed to complement one another. Never was it intended by God that they should worship differently. All of the laws were for the whole nation and the punishments levied were on the entire nation. They were all Israel. Only after the death of Solomon would an artificial schism in the Hebrews come and it was a direct reason for their ultimate fall and dispersion of the nation later on.

In an automobile there are hundreds of parts with most being very different in appearance and function that must be connected in order to work. They must fit together in order for all of the different forces to complement each other making the car travel in the direction and at the speed necessary. All of the people of God both those of Israel in the past and the Church in the present must complement and draw strength from each other and stay connected in order for the purpose to be fulfilled.

God knows that there are many things that make us different from each other – nationality, generation, race, gender, culture and subculture, political loyalties and many other less conspicuous reasons. But none of these distinctives are reasons to divide us, they are simply God's design to make us better fit His purpose and fit together with each other. Black and white should not be in a different mindset because their color or their culture is different. There should not be "churches" designed to cater to young people or old people or rich people or poor people, city people or country people. As a matter of fact there shouldn't be churches in the traditional sense of the word at all. Our nomenclature is all wrong in that we say "churches" rather than "the Church." We say "my pastor" rather than "a pastor." We say Black church or white church, Hispanic or oriental church like there was actually, biblically such a thing. These are an abomination as we are all the Church!

It is possible to be distinct but yet still be unified if we are obedient to the Word. However, the history of the organized Church has been "turf oriented" since shortly after its beginning. The day of Pentecost was a miraculous day in that all who would believe would be grafted into the new, living thing known as the *"ekklesia,"* the *"called out."* Christ had died not just to save individuals but also to give birth to the Church that would proclaim His glory over the earth. There was a beautiful life with growth coming from God in response to the obedience of His children. The book of Acts is full of the organic life of the Church producing converts, churches (fellowships – home gatherings of believers) then the converts multiplying in number as they multiplied in the knowledge of God and then Churches multiplying. It was a natural process that God and His children were functioning in together.

Look at the progression:

> *"And they* (the believers), *continuing daily with one accord in the temple and breaking bread from house to house, did eat their meat with gladness and singleness of heart, praising God, and having favor with all the people. And the Lord added to the church daily such as should be saved.*
>
> *Acts 2:46-47(KJV)*
>
> *"And believers were the more added to the Lord, multitudes of both men and women. Insomuch that they brought forth the sick into the streets, and laid them on beds and couches, that at the least the shadow of Peter passing by might overshadow some of them.*
>
> *Acts 5:14-15(KJV)*
>
> *"And the word of God increased and the number of the disciples multiplied in Jerusalem greatly; and a great company of the priests were obedient to the faith."*
>
> *Acts 6:7(KJV)*

Notice that things are happening in Judea and Galilee and Samaria and not just in Jerusalem. The power of the Word of God is expanding but nothing would indicate that the organic unity was breaking down.

> *"Then had the churches* (the gatherings of believers – not churches as we think of them today) *rest throughout all Judea and Galilee and Samaria, and were edified; and walking in the fear of the Lord, and in the comfort of the Holy Ghost, were multiplied."*
>
> *Acts 9:31(KJV)*

> *"And the hand of the Lord was with them: and a great number believed and turned unto the Lord."*
> Acts 11:21(KJV)

The influence and the impact of the Word was growing:

> *"But the word of God grew and multiplied."*
> Acts 12:24(KJV)

We are almost ready to see the climax of what God was doing in our next verse:

> *"And so were the churches established in the faith, and increased in number daily.*
> Acts 16:5(KJV)

And here is the ultimate point, the place that every generation of believers in every place should expect:

> *"So mightily grew the word of God and prevailed."*
> Acts 20:20(KJV)

Acts 20:20 is the ultimate and the people of God must have 20:20 vision!

Would you think that the unity in the Church would grow out of the work of God in their culture? Verses 42 through 47 of Chapter 2 are the sweetest words of fellowship that I have ever read. They were in one accord. They shared their time and their living. Even though they were different, their hearts beat as one. The unity came first and everything came as a result of God working through that oneness. This is how it must come for us also. We must make a conscious effort to cast away the things that have historically divided us and grab onto the common faith. We must have the same heart and love.

Chapter 7

A City Wide Church

Think of how many times in scripture a Church is named by the city in which the people live; the Church at Jerusalem, Antioch, Ephesus, Corinth, Rome, Colosse, Phillippi, Thessalonica, Laodicea, Smyrna, Philadelphia, Pergamos, Thyatira, Sardis and the region of Galatia. We hear of Lyda, Iconium and many others.

In the right dividing of the Word, one of the most important principles is to understand who is being spoken to. For instance, the book of Romans is written *"to all in Rome who are loved of God and called to be saints."* Romans is written to the Church at Rome and their special circumstances but also applies to the Church in every time and every place. Written to the body of Christ also are the books of Corinthians, Galatians, Ephesians, Philippians, Colossians, I & II Thessalonians, I & II Peter and the three letters of John. The letters to the seven Churches in Revelation 2&3 show very clearly that the risen Christ is concerned with the corporate character of the churches in the different cities.

What separates and distinguishes a body of believers? It is the city, and in a few instances the region in which they live and minister that groups believers together. When the Lord of Glory and the great apostles to the Jews and Gentiles, Peter and Paul, address their remarks specifically to a group of believers in a geo-political entity, we must take special note of the reason. It is imperative that we also study whether this would have any significance to us today. First though let's look at the issue of corporate character.

When Jesus speaks to the seven churches in Revelation 2&3, He speaks either commendation or condemnation. To the church at Ephesus Christ proclaims:

> *"I know your deeds, your hard work and your perseverance. I know that you cannot tolerate wicked men, that you have tested those who claim to be apostles but are not, and have found them false. You have persevered and have endured hardship for my name, and have grown weary.*
>
> *Yet I hold this against you: you have forsaken your first love. Remember the height from which you have fallen. Repent and do the things you did at first. If you do not repent, I will come and remove your lampstand from its place. But you have this in your favor: you hate the practices of the Nicolaitans which I also hate."*
>
> Revelation 2:2-7

Jesus is not speaking to individual believers but to a body. He is not saying "all of you are guilty of losing your first love" nor is He saying "all of you work hard and persevere" but rather says, "This is your character as a group."

Throughout church history there have been people who showed by their walk the glory of Christ at work in a person. Extra-biblically we have the record of their lives. *"Foxes' Book of Martyrs"* records the supreme sacrifice given as an offering to God by His most giving of servants; those that "*... were tortured, not accepting deliverance; that they might obtain a better resurrection.*" *Hebrews 11:35b(KJV)* We know from the struggles leading to the Protestant Reformation that many gave the full measure for the establishment of the doctrine of salvation by grace through faith as opposed to a salvation by works. The giants of the faith are everywhere through the chronicles of history but where is the corporate greatness that appears to be the point of Christ's establishment of His church on this earth?

I make the proposition here that there has not been a time since the rise of Emperor Constantine and the Christianization of the world that the church has approached the intent that God has had for His people. If the day of Pentecost was the birthday of the church then where should we be two thousand years later? Should we not be a maturing adult ready to be presented as a spotless bride by the Son to the Father? Should the world not be a different place because we are here? Since 324 AD the church has been characterized by Cain-like activities. Vain religion is our offering! Cain's way is the way of the broken cistern: taking what is our idea of the glory of God and preserving it. The world sees it! Only a confrontational look in our mirror with the heart to change and be obedient will ever facilitate God using us to bring His glory to the earth!

A city-wide church is the biblical prototype for the living Church of today. Our structure much be defined by the city in which God has placed us and our qualities as a body must be defined in reference to the city in which we live. Listen to what *Acts 17:10-11* say about the Jews in Berea:

> "*And the brethren* (in Thessalonica) *immediately sent away Paul and Silas by night unto Berea: who coming hither went into the synagogue of the Jews. These were more noble than those in Thessalonica, in that they received the word with*

all readiness of mind and searched the scriptures daily, whether those things were so."

(KJV)

Paul's point of reference for all commendations and condemnations was always the city and the group of people in it.

When Christ and Paul addressed the church in the different cities, their purpose was to establish them. They were looking at the different qualities, faults and failures of these different bodies with the purpose of making them into a people that would show the glory of the Lord to the earth and to succeeding generations. The purpose was that the people of God would become the habitation of God, established in the faith, passing down the purity of love for Christ and from Christ from generation to generation; a dwelling place for the glory of God.

In Acts 20:17, Paul, in Ephesus, calls for the elders of the church to come to him at Miletus in order to give them words of encouragement and direction. The elders came from all over the city. They were leaders of the body of Christ and also the leaders in the smaller house churches. The church at Ephesus was unified to the extent that the local fellowships were able to function together on a city wide level. They were exhibiting community traits and these traits developed and changed over the life of the Church.

For any group of people, be it social, political or cultural, there must be boundaries. There must be some means of distinguishing between them, not to divide them but to unite them. Biblically this is cities. Hopefully there will be a day when the church that we identify with will be the church in New York, Cleveland, Los Angeles, Omaha, Charleston, Grand Rapids, etc.

Recently I asked a minister friend of mine what city church he identified with. The church he pastors is almost equidistant between our states' two largest cities, Charleston and Huntington, West Virginia but maybe a little closer to Charleston. He said that he was definitely identified with Charleston. When I pressed him as to why, he couldn't answer anything other than that is what he felt in his heart. The Holy Spirit is the one that told him because the Holy Spirit determines our Church. We are directed by God to be part of the body He has decided for us and He has gifted us and chosen us to function within that body. Because of this the choice is no longer ours as to where we go even if we are "doing" the things that He has called us to do. If we are not functioning in our call and in the city wide church He has called us to then we are out of His order.

If the church in a city is the biblical prototype then everything possible must be done to recognize it and once again make it the pattern. What must change, what must go in order for that to happen?

Denomination

In looking at God's plan for the organization of His people, and seeing the truth of a city wide church, we must now look at what has happened to break down God's arrangement. Whenever man begins to build something on his own, he makes sure that he justifies it. In the case of disunity in the church, Christianity has declared that there are reasons that we should be divided. There are cultural differences that make it impractical or impossible for us to function together. We have taken minor doctrinal differences and determined that there is full reason to be separate from other believers because of them. The beautiful pattern for conflict resolution that we see in Acts 15 over the circumcision issue is evidence that the pattern was to work out differences, not split over them but in our zeal to fashion broken cisterns, we have rejected reconciliation and unity.

The Jews and the Gentiles of the first century were the greatest schism between people that could be imagined. The Jews considered that they were the objects of salvation, missing the reality that they were being used by God to reach all mankind.

Ephesians 3:4-5 reveals what God was doing. Paul says, *"Whereby when ye read, ye may understand my knowledge in the mystery of Christ, which in other ages was not made known unto the sons of men, as it is now revealed unto his holy apostles and prophets by the spirit; that the Gentiles should be fellow heirs of the same body, and partakers of his promise in Christ by the gospel... " (KJV)*

God, through Christ, had made all men one through the Spirit, *"Having abolished in his flesh the enmity, even the law of commandments contained in ordinances; for to make in himself of twain one new man, so making peace... " Ephesians 2:15(KJV)* He made all men one and through that oneness came peace. The peace comes from us being *"one new man"* and unless we remain *"one new man,"* the peace is conditional. Unless we live out, unless we choose to look like what we are, we will not manifest what He has made us. Just like we were made righteous, justified and sanctified through Christ at our new birth, God has told us throughout His Word that we are to live like what He has made us! *"Walk worthy of the vocation wherewith ye were called"* we are told in Ephesians

> *"And that he might reconcile both* (Jews and Gentiles) *unto God in one body by the cross having slain the enmity thereby... "*
> *Eph 2:16(KJV)*

God, through Christ's cross, took the greatest division between people and broke it down but we have built it back up again because of our carnal desire to build our own systems. The beauty of what God did in Christ has been rejected by the church in favor of a system, a cistern that can hold no water. It has been with us so long that we feel that it is impossible to live without and most Christians actually think that it is part of what God did at Pentecost. What I refer to is denomination.

Artificial divisions in the body of Christ are exactly that – divisions. Whenever believers are separated spiritually there is error and disobedience that leads to distance from God. What people are able to do though, is learn how to live with error. This is where the church is now, in the twenty-first century. We have learned to live with an artificial division that has no basis in scripture and breaks the heart of God.

Whenever a couple is married in a church, the minister will say to them just after the pronouncement that "what God has joined together, let not man separate." Yet in a zeal to "do the work of the Lord," we have let man separate us. Denomination has said that because of differences in our cultures or our traditions and even our backgrounds, we should be separate. Because I am white and you are black it wouldn't be feasible for us to be together as Christians or so we think even if we aren't willing to say it.

Denomination is diametrically opposed to the unity of the body of Christ and the city wide church, not intentionally, mind you, but by its nature. Instead of banding together organically in the places that God has placed us, we go to believers of other cities and work with them. We use the excuse that they are more culturally or doctrinally in tune with how we feel – we are more comfortable with them. God grieves! His heart breaks because the unifying power of the cross of Jesus Christ has been made null and void on a corporate level. Oh, we are still saved but the power of the church is lost. What God had intended to bring us to the greatness of Pentecost has been rejected. We have rejected the fountain of living waters and instead taken little palms full of water and taken them to the cisterns, broken cisterns that we have built. The water leaks out and stagnates and we somehow learn to live with it. It's OK because that is simply the way things are. For us it is satisfactory to just have a little rather than have it all.

The church has learned to live with the modus operandi of going into peoples lives after the enemy has ravaged them rather than being the habitation of the Lord where we influence the culture. Rather than being an army that comes into a village after it has been plundered we should be standing strong in protection of the culture not allowing the enemy in. This is God's intention! Instead of condemning sin in those who have never believed we should be looking at the sin in the church and finding out where it is coming from. Why are our children leaving the church as soon as they are old enough to make their own decisions?

The world has influenced this denomination based "church" rather than the other way around. Our methods are the world's methods. We are organizational rather than organic. We are a corporate structure rather than a *"building fitly framed together"* that *"growth unto a holy temple in the Lord: in whom ye are also builded together for a habitation of God through the Spirit." Eph. 2:21-22(KJV)*

Denomination cannot be anything other than a business structure that sucks the life out of true community. It has become by its nature the end rather than a means to an end. "I'm Church of God, Methodist, Catholic, Southern Baptist, ad infinitum..." the people of God say, while the differences between Christians grows wider and the difference between what has been built and the true blood bought church of Jesus Christ do not even remotely resemble one another. (Consider *Acts 2:42-47*)

The spruced up religion of Cain shows itself in our world as the denominational church. Our offerings to God are planned and programmed rather than flowing naturally out of love for Him and community with each other. Our structure perverts the plan of God to preserve the natural unity of people in true worship and ministry. Under denomination, we have an excuse for being divided. The church can take minor doctrinal differences and on that basis separate ourselves from each other. We can say, "I love you but based on our differences I can't function with you. You do your thing and we'll do ours. There are people in a different city that think like we do so we'll get together with them." It propagates and perpetuates division. Whenever there is a problem that should be worked out, we can just decide to form our own organization and leave others to form theirs. We look at this as simply "the way things are" but I put before you the theory that this is the very reason that the church is impotent, powerless and contributes to the fact that for the most part the world is dying and headed to hell. The religious establishment *has "hewn themselves cisterns, broken cisterns that can hold no water."* There is a form of godliness that denies the power of God. This power is denied covertly rather than overtly in that for the most part Christians are ignorant of the problem. How can you miss something you never had? The essence is that we have been robbed by our carnal, corporate nature of the true organic being called the Church and opted for an organization called church.

There is before us a container of our own making that will not hold what God wants to give. God gives gifts for a city church and we use them in the small local fellowship or in the large national/international organization. The true city church is skipped, ignored and the biblical model is hardly recognized or understood.

Apostles, prophets, evangelists and pastor teachers are functioning so far out of their anointing and call that when they are looked at in the context of today's system, they are hardly recognizable. We will talk more about this in the chapter title **"Misplaced Gifts."**

The Christians in a city, all being led by different organizations, are unfruitful, confused, unproductive and fragmented and in many cases, ignorant of the basic spiritual needs of the community around them. There should be natural Christian relationships developing in each city that prevent anyone in need from falling between the cracks or duplication of ministry also. I am not talking about feeding the poor or housing the homeless but about having the love of Jesus Christ seen by the city. All of the good deeds should flow from that.

Missionaries should be raised up and sent out by the body of Christ where you and I live not by a multi national conglomerate. The fellowships in a city where the missionaries come from should be supporting them with prayer, some finances and volunteer help. There needs to be hands on, relational contact between the senders and the sent.

The denominational monstrosities are receiving money from local congregations and the money is divvied up and then sent back to the local churches both at home and abroad. If this system worked, if it were the biblical model, then the world would surely have had the chance to accept or reject Jesus by now.

> *"And this continued by the space of two years; so that all they which dwelt in Asia heard the word of the Lord Jesus, both Jews and Greeks."*
> *Acts 19:10(KJV)*

What happened to make the whole of Asia hear the word of the Lord? It was nothing other than believers living in community and all the gifts of the Lord being lived out by the people who had received those gifts. Paul was an apostle and a teacher and that is what he did. Wherever he went he taught and ministered. He was received by the Church because he was an apostle to the entire body of Christ, not just some fragment of it. Paul had relationships with the people because he was recognized by the leadership as being the man of God. There was a network of complete Christian bodies in the different cities, not just pieces here and pieces there. Think of "a Paul" being raised up by God in our day. Who would he be presented to? If he came into a town under the auspices of the Southern Baptists, would he ever be heard by the Methodists? If he wrote a doctrinal letter, who would he send it to? How would anyone other than a small segment get to read it? This is at the root of the problem in the twenty-first century Church.

There can be no other reason to criticize denomination other than it doesn't work. It is the result of an unbiblical, religious desire to fashion our own system. It is a "broken cistern that can hold no water."

God calls for, no, demands unity. It is to be part of our changed nature, it is to be the result of us living in intimacy with Him and when the oneness isn't there, it is symptomatic of our division. It is impossible for Him to work! But what the people of God decide to do as a result of God not working is that we work in His place – not with Him, being fellow-laborers, but instead of Him. Most of what we see in the structure of the church today is what we have decided to build because "He isn't working." I don't mean that He is not at work just that we are not at work with Him. He's over there, we're over here. He's doing this, we're doing that. It grieves Him, it breaks His heart. It is evil, *"for my people have committed two evils..."*

Chapter 8

The Work of the Holy Spirit

A glaring weakness of our "broken cisterns" is the fact that in the organized church, the leading and guiding of the body has come from within, without the Holy Spirit having much to do with anything. We are so used to making our own decisions that we have come to ignore the possibility that He is waiting to lead our every move.

Our Lord Jesus Christ addressed His disciples on the night of His arrest and told them this:

> *"But now I go my way to him that sent me; and none of you asketh me, Wither goest thou? But because I have said these things unto you, sorrow hath filled your heart. Nevertheless I tell you the truth; It is expedient that I go away: for if I go not away, the Comforter will not come unto you; but if I depart I will send him unto you."*
>
> *John 16:5-7(KJV)*

In His comforting of these men who trusted Him implicitly, He told them that there would be One that would come to take His place; to do the things that He did.

The way they walked behind Jesus they would follow the Holy Spirit. But there would be one difference: *"for he dwelleth with you, **and shall be in you.**"* John 14:17b(KJV) The Lord was saying that a day was coming when not only will the Spirit be with them but a day is coming when the Spirit will indwell them; the Spirit will live inside of them and all who throughout this dispensation call upon the name of the Lord for salvation. Something more than the baptism of John awaits those who repent; something more than the power of the flesh, human ability, awaits believers in Christ. There is a new knowledge and wisdom that is poised to witness to the world and this power is not just for you and I individually but is for us collectively!

> *"But ye shall receive power, after the Holy Ghost is come upon you: and ye shall be witnesses unto me both in Jerusalem, and in all Judea, and in Samaria, and unto the uttermost part of the earth."*
> Acts 1:8(KJV)

Because Jesus died and was raised again, the Holy Spirit came as the *"promise of the Father" (v4)*. The Spirit gave power to minister and transform the earth, to witness the truth of the Gospel of Jesus Christ – and men have been denying Him and ignoring Him ever since! Instead, what the church has attempted to do is all of the things that Jesus commanded but in our own strength and our own abilities, forsaking a yielding to the true power. The church has set up an organizational structure rather than follow the leading of the Spirit. It is akin to Moses and his realization of the plight of his Hebrew countrymen leading him to take matters into his own hands by killing the bully Egyptian. It is like David taking it upon himself to build a house to bring glory to the Lord. It reminds one of Gideon being taught by the Lord

Himself to pare down his earthly forces and submit to God's way and power. The Bible is full of examples that teach a lesson that is hardly learned; a lesson that has cost the mortal souls of millions. God has the plan and the power and we have replaced it with a plan that costs us little; a plan that we ourselves can control. It is control that must be given up in order for the power to have free course.

"But ye shall receive power... " Getting back to the power that Jesus died to make available, it must be said that this power, *dunamis,* in the Greek is an inherent power that must be activated. It is where our word dynamite comes from and it can just sit there doing nothing should its bearers so desire – we have so desired. We have said "no" to lighting the fuse, "no" to placing it right in the world where it will make a difference. We have denied that we have it and once you see it at work it will break your heart that we have been so idolatrous. Once the miraculous work of God is experienced it can no longer be denied.

Shortly after Pentecost, Peter and John are walking into the Temple through the Beautiful gate and they see a lame man. *"Silver and gold have I none,"* Peter says, *"but such as I have give I thee: In the name of Jesus of Nazareth, rise up and walk." Acts 3:6(KJV)* He did! He walked! And Peter tells the people gathered in the Temple, *"Ye men of Israel, why marvel ye at this? Or why look ye so earnestly on us, as though by our own power or holiness we had made this man to walk?(v12) (KJV)* It wasn't anything to do with them or their power but it was the Holy Spirit operating through them. This is the result of Pentecost.

The church of today should be no different than the body of believers that lived and walked two thousand years ago. These same two men, Peter and John had, before the day of Pentecost, *"... when the doors were shut where the disciples were assembled for fear of the Jew... "* been hiding, cowering in terror. Something happened to them; they were now confident and focused, knowing that they were filled with a new strength and boldness. Jesus had died and was raised again to empower His followers to be His witnesses in every corner of the world.

The question that must be asked by believers today is: Does this power still exist and are Christians its recipients and its conduits? As I search Scripture I do not see anything to indicate that the answer to this question is that we are not. There is a clear break in Acts at the rejection of the Jews to the Gospel and a focus change to the Gentiles but the method is still the same – power. Paul talks about the Spirit's power to further the Gospel when he is addressing the Gentile believers in Corinth. *"And my speech and my preaching was not with enticing words of man's wisdom, but in demonstration of the Spirit and of power." I Corinthians 2:4(KJV)*

It is not words spoken by human beings in skillful ways that change people but it is the force of the Spirit through their words and actions.

> *"For I am not ashamed of the gospel of Christ: for it is the power of God unto salvation to everyone that believeth; to the Jew first, and also to the Greeks* (Gentiles).
>
> *Romans 1:16 (KJV)*

Everyone who accepts Christ in faith is a vehicle by which the power of the Gospel is conveyed to the world.

Can the Gospel be preached to the earth without the power of the Holy Spirit behind it, backing it, enforcing it, enabling it? The verse quoted above, *I Corinthians 2:4*, has already provided us with a satisfactory answer. *"And my speech and my preaching was not with enticing words of man's wisdom,* **but** *in demonstration of the Spirit and of power."*

The biggest little word in the English language is *but* because it contrasts the phrase before with the phrase after. The contrast here is between *enticing words* and *man's wisdom* with the *demonstration of the Spirit* and *power.* We can conclude logically that all of the enticing words of man's wisdom do not necessarily demonstrate God's power and can therefore have little effect. In a detailed examination of Church history, since the early church, there has been little power. If there had been, it could be safely assumed that the world would be a considerably different place; the word of God could have been trusted like in Acts 19:20 to have grown *"mightily"* and *"prevailed."* There is even a statement in *verse 10* of the same chapter: *"And this continued* (Paul's teachings in Ephesus) *by the space of two years; so that all they which dwelt in Asia heard the word of the Lord Jesus, both Jews and Greeks." (KJV)* Most of the civilized world heard the Word.

Something has hindered the Spirit's work through the church. What is it? What has happened?

The Spirit Speaks

> *"Now there were in the church that was at Antioch certain prophets and teachers; as Barnabas and Simeon that was called Niger, and Lucius of Cyrene, and Manaen, which had been brought up with Herod the tetrarch, and Saul. As they ministered to the Lord, and fasted,* **the Holy Ghost said***, Separate me Barnabas and Saul for the work whereunto I have called them. And when they had fasted and prayed, and laid their hands on them, they sent them away."*
> *Acts 13:1-3(KJV)*

There is the tendency in people to hear things so often that the details of what they hear are missed. Or they also have the inclination to ignore what they don't think is important even to the point of subconsciously denying its reality. The reality in *Acts 13:1-3* is that *"... the Holy Ghost said..."* The Holy Ghost said...! How often does the church today actually hear the Holy Spirit speak? This is not the only place where He spoke either:

> *"And now, behold, I go bound in the spirit unto Jerusalem, not knowing the things that shall befall me there: Save that the Holy Ghost witnesseth in every city, **saying** that, bonds and afflictions abide me."*
> *Acts 20:22-23(KJV)*
>
> *"And when he was come unto us* (Agabus the prophet), *he took Paul's girdle, and bound his own hands and feet, and said, Thus **saith** the Holy Ghost, So shall the Jews at Jerusalem bind the man that owneth this girdle, and shall deliver him into the hands of the Gentiles."*
> *Acts 21:11(KJV)*

There are many other references to the direct leadership of the Holy Spirit over the people of God in the early church. Where is it now? Do we miss it? Are we suffering because of our usurpation of the responsibility of the Holy Spirit (God) over the actions of the church? Has it cost the world the witness of Christ? The answer to all of these questions is a resounding "Yes"! How could we have ever thought that we could possibly do things better than God? In our zeal to "do," we have neglected to "be" submissive to His will and have soundly rejected Him except as a "rubber stamp" for what we have already decided.

The "headship" of Christ over the church is ministered by the One whom Jesus sent, the Comforter, the Helper, the Strengthener, the One who would *"... teach you all things, and bring all things to your remembrance, whatsoever I have said to you."* John 14:26b(KJV)

He will very seldom say the things that we expect Him to and this has been a source of reluctance to hear Him. The Spirit leads contrary to the flesh and we enjoy and trust the flesh. We are comfortable with what the flesh tells because it appears to be logical. However, Paul makes it clear in his letter to the Romans that: *"... I know that in me (that is, in my flesh,) dwelleth no good thing: for to will is present with me; but how to perform that which is good I find not."* Romans 7:18(KJV) This is not just an individual problem but also a corporate problem. We are not able to do more alone than we are together and are just as disobedient either way.

Here is the remedy:

> *"For if ye live after the flesh, ye shall die: but if ye through the Sprit do mortify* (blow up, explode) *the deeds of the body, ye shall live. For as many are led by the Spirit of God, they are the sons of God. For ye have not received the spirit of bondage again to fear; but ye have received the Spirit of adoption, whereby we cry, Abba, Father. The Spirit itself bear witness with our spirit, that we are the children of God."*
> Romans 8:13-16(KJV)

We must first acknowledge the fact that there is a problem with counting on the flesh rather than the Spirit. The next thing is that we must stop doing it! "Blow up" what we do in our own wisdom and strength; seek to do only what the Spirit leads us to and live in the loving relationship that

God has called us to when He adopted us as His own children. The word *Abba* indicates intimacy and love and should be at the heart of what we are as Christians. Everything that we do should flow out of what we are; the leadership of the Spirit should not have to be sought but should be a part of our relationship with the Father. The Spirit is who the Father uses to communicate with His children. The Spirit is the One who will smash our "broken cisterns."

The same way that the disciples followed Jesus, we are to follow the Holy Ghost. Where He goes, we go; what He directs is what we do; what He teaches, we learn and basically watch Him bring the results. Ninety nine percent of what the modern church does is done in our own wisdom and strength and all of the failures are laid at our feet. The lost are everywhere and many are still lost because the Holy Spirit has not been heard and obeyed and the power of the Gospel has not been shown. We are responsible! Just as Israel was intended to be a beacon to the nations in the generations before Christ, showing a waiting world the abilities of God working through an obedient people, we, the church, are to be so now. **A sinful world is condemned by us for its sinfulness when we are the reason that they have never heard.** If only we would act as much like what we really are as they do, everything would be better. God would be pleased with us.

You and I individually and even more, you and I together, must hear from God.

There have been times in my ministry when I have ministered in my own power, according to my own plan and then there have been times that I have seen miracles in ministry done by the Holy Spirit through me. The difference was so profound and I never have had any doubt either way knowing what was going on. It is always beautiful to behold when He is at work and pitiful when it is I. I will seek to never do things on my own, even at the risk of doing nothing, at the expense of watching His magnificent work. He heals! He saves! He transforms!

How many decisions in "the Church" are made by councils and committees sitting around a table, sharing information, coming to conclusions and making plans for the implementation of those conclusions? These are sound business practices but have no place in the New Testament Church. We have already read about how the Holy Spirit spoke to the Church in *Acts 13:1-3 (KJV)* but what else happened there?

"Now there were in the church that was in Antioch certain prophets and teachers; as Barnabas, and Simeon that was called Niger, and Lucius of Cyrene, and Manaen, which had been brought up with Herod the tetrarch and Saul. As they ministered to the Lord, and fasted, the Holy Ghost said, "Separate me Barnabas and Saul for the work whereunto I have called them. " And when they had fasted and prayed, and laid their hands on them, they sent them away.

The first thing is that we must recognize that there were *teachers* and *prophets* in the Church. The gifts were being operated by those whom the Spirit had anointed. The Church was fasting as they ministered in their daily lives. (*The Greek word for "ministered" in this verse means "public work."*) They prayed and went about their lives until they got an answer. This is the prototype for the operation of the Holy Spirit in the life of the corporate body of believers. After the answer was heard, the Church laid their hands on Barnabas and Saul and agreeing with the Spirit's decision, sent them out.

What has taken us away from looking at our decisions in this way? The fact is that 90% of our decisions have little or nothing to do with the work of God in the first place. We ask Him to help us decide how to do things He never led us to do in the first place. It's backwards.

Dependence is the optimum word for the life of the Church in our day or in any day, total dependence, with the only things we do being instigated by Him, enabled by Him and followed through by Him. He gives answers. He gives strength and more than anything, He gives power.

There Is No Other Way

> *"Verily, verily, I say unto you, He that believeth on me, the works that I do shall he do also; and greater works than these shall he do; because I go unto my Father."*
>
> *John 14:12(KJV)*

John 14:12 is one of the most important dispensational verses in the Bible. It tells us that Jesus was going away and because He was leaving and going back to the Father by way of crucifixion, burial and resurrection, He was ushering in a new time; a time in which the power that He showed would be matched and exceeded in scope by those that would believe in Him. I didn't write it or say it, I'm just telling you what Jesus said. How often has the Church acted like this verse was the truth? How long have we considered that Jesus was telling *"he that believeth"* in Him that we would do greater works than His? And how much have we considered the reasons why we don't live up to His prophetic statement?

Only in walking in the power of the Spirit will we see the world changed. If we walk in the wisdom of the flesh, which is all that's available without the Spirit, we will be full of fear and trepidation just like the disciples shortly after Jesus' resurrection.

> *"Then the same day at evening, being the first day of the week, when the doors were shut where the disciples were assembled **for fear of the Jews,***

came Jesus and stood in the midst, and saith unto them, "Peace be unto you."
> John 20:19(KJV)

Just as His closest disciples scattered on the night of His capture, just as Peter had denied Him those times, they were gathered in this room in terror for their own lives. They had not yet been empowered. They were still in the dispensation of the law. What Jesus had come to make fully available was not yet. They were told to *"wait for the promise of the Father."* Wait at Jerusalem, they were told. There would be something coming that would change them and enable them to be His witnesses.

> *"But ye shall receive power, after that the Holy Ghost is come upon you; and ye shall be witnesses unto me both in Jerusalem, and in all Judea, and in Samaria, and unto the uttermost part of the earth."*
> Acts 1:8(KJV)

Then it happened! Some fifty days after the resurrection on the Feast of Pentecost, the Feast of Weeks, came the promise!

> *"And when the day of Pentecost was fully come, they were all with one accord in one place. And suddenly there came a sound from heaven as of a rushing mighty wind, and it filled the house where they were sitting. And there appeared unto them cloven tongues like as of fire, and it sat upon each of them. And they were all filled with the Holy Ghost, and began to speak with other tongues, as the Spirit gave them utterance"*
> Acts 2:1-4(KJV)

There you have it! A new dispensation! The Church age and the age of grace had been ushered in. Its character would be a time of power and ministry, or so God intended. If allowed, the Spirit would grab hold of the willing disciple and minister through him.

> *"Ye men of Israel, hear these words,; Jesus of Nazareth, a man approved of God among you by miracles and wonders and signs, which God did by him in the midst of you, as ye yourselves also know: Him being delivered by the determinate counsel and foreknowledge of God, ye have taken and by wicked hands have crucified and slain..."*
>
> *(KJV)*

Notice that this is one of the men who seven weeks prior had been hiding behind closed doors for fear of the people that he was now pointing his finger at and accusing of crucifying the Lord. This was a changed man! Something had happened in his nature and he wasn't the only one. They were all changed; all who had received the gift that day and since were changed. You and I have received the gift as a result of our faith and the same power should be working through us.

The radical event that had changed the people of God from simply being followers of Jesus to being followers of Christ, indwelt and empowered by the Comforter had come. The Promise was now here. The Spirit was no longer "upon" men but was now "in" men.

> *"And I will pray the Father, and he shall give you another Comforter, that he may abide with you forever; even the Spirit of truth; whom the world cannot receive, because it seeth him not, neither*

*knoweth him: but ye know him; for he dwelleth with you, **and shall be in you.***"
John 14:16-17(KJV)

My friends, nothing of any eternal value can be done without Him.

"Nevertheless I tell you the truth; It is expedient for you that I go away: for if I go not away, the Comforter will not come unto you; but if I depart, I will send him unto you. And when he is come, he will reprove the world of sin, and of righteousness, and of judgment: Of sin, because they believe not on me; Of righteousness, because I go to my Father, and ye see me no more; Of judgment, because the prince of this world is judged."
John 16:7-11(KJV)

The world is convicted of sin, not because of anything we say but because of what He does. The world sees righteousness by being effected by those that have been filled by the Holy Spirit allowing Him to show Himself through them. Because Jesus went to the Father, the world has the example of righteousness before them. The world and Satan and his systems are judged – found guilty at Calvary, sentenced to death. The Spirit has the power to show this to all who wonder and also to show the glory of the resurrection to all who search. Had Satan and his forces have known all that would come from Jesus' death, burial and resurrection, he wouldn't have been behind Jesus' death.

"But we speak the wisdom of God in a mystery, even the hidden wisdom, which God ordained before the world unto our glory: Which none of the princes of this world knew: for had they

known it, they would not have crucified the Lord of glory."

I Corinthians 2:7-8(KJV)

The Church has walked in the wisdom of this world, man's wisdom that has resulted in the implementation of man's ideas and programs. This has resulted in a world that is desperate and dying. Everything that we can think of to further the cause of Christ results in marginal results, not the earth shaking power-filled work of the Holy Ghost through the Church. Yes, people do get saved. *"Even a blind squirrel finds a hickory nut every once-in-a-while."* God still sends those that search to His people for the good news but what about societal transformation and spiritual awakening? In order for this to happen, we are not to "do" anything but we are to "be" something.

Being Not Doing

The Old Testament contains the record of God's dealings with mankind leading up to the redemption of the earth through Jesus Christ. He begins by forming a people, a race, who He would use to show Himself to the world. As other peoples' watched God's dealing with Israel, they would know that there was a great God who was personally concerned about human beings. They would see God through His dealings with the Hebrew race and know that the gods made with men's hands were not gods at all. Unless He showed Himself, they would never know

God built the nation of Israel through Abraham, Isaac and Jacob and grew them up in the land of Goshen in Egypt until He heard their cries from slavery and delivered them through Moses. He led them through the wilderness and to the shores of the Red Sea with Pharaoh's army in hot pursuit. But even in the hopelessness of that situation

He revealed His power in the parting of the sea. We must realize that not just Israel would hear about this miraculous feat but it would be noised throughout the world for the rest of history. As Israel walked in the desert, other nations saw them or heard about them and just in the simple fact that they were fed, watered and clothed was a miracle that must have spread everywhere. How could these people survive in conditions such as these? Every nation had a national god or gods and Israel's God must be very powerful.

Jehovah fed them with manna, gave them water from the rocks, their shoes didn't wear out and they had left Egypt with enough valuables to do what God was planning in the building of the Tabernacle. They were not asked to do anything but just be His people and let Him be their God. Moses had no idea what to do at the seashore until they got to the seashore. They knew not where the water would come from until they needed water, the same with food. They didn't know that their shoes wouldn't wear out until their shoes didn't wear out.

Should the Church be the same? Are we now the people of God with the same principles involved in our purpose? Are we to be allowing Him to show Himself through us, by His actions and not ours? When we look at the Bible from cover to cover, I believe that it is obvious that Israel is our prototype. They show us how the people of God at any time are to allow God to receive glory through what He does for us and not what we do for Him. It is a very subtle difference but a very important difference. It is the difference between truth and error and could explain the fruitlessness of the Church through the millennia since Christ's sacrifice. A yielding to the leadership of the Holy Spirit would show us collectively that He will do miracles through us that the world would be forced to recognize. They will not be the kind of wonders that we expect but a new work, a new way. He is only waiting for us to obey.

He is only waiting for us to obey! We cry out as if He has turned His back on us but it is we that have turned our backs on Him.

As God's Spirit leads His people, they are to learn and trust. As each move of God is less logical to our senses, we see that it must be God. Why didn't God lead Israel around the Red Sea? Why did He pare down Gideon's forces? Why didn't Isaac come to Abraham and Sarah when they were young rather than very old? Why was a virgin called to give birth to the Messiah?

But the Church goes along making logical, business-like plans for the winning of the world and it doesn't seem to work. It doesn't work because God doesn't tell His people to "do," He tells them to "be."

> *"I will be your God and you will be My people."*

Listen to what He tells the Church in the book of Ephesians:

> *"But now in Christ Jesus ye who sometimes were far off are made nigh by the blood of Christ."*
> 2:13(KJV)

He did it! He bridges the gap. He reconciled us through the blood of His Son.

> *"For he is our peace, who hath made both one, and hath broken down the middle wall of partition between us."*
> 2:14(KJV)

He did it! He gave us our peace. He made Jew and Gentile the same family, both sons and daughters. There is no more inherent division in man.

> *"Having abolished in his flesh the enmity, even the law of commandments contained in ordinances; for to make of himself of twain one new man, so making peace."*
>
> *2:15(KJV)*

He did it! He fulfilled the law through Christ; the law had condemned us but the judgment of guilt at Calvary was also the moment of payment. He judged us guilty but at the same time paid the price of redemption. He did it!

> *"And that he might reconcile both unto God in one body by the cross, having slain the enmity thereby: And came and preached peace to you who were afar off, and to them who were nigh. For through him we both have access by one Spirit unto the Father."*
>
> *2:16-18(KJV)*

He did it! He made all one no matter where we have our roots. Near or far He has made us one.

> *"Now therefore ye are no more strangers and foreigners, but fellow citizens with the saints, and of the household of God. And are built upon the foundation of the apostles and prophets, Jesus Christ himself being the chief corner stone;"*
>
> *2:19-20(KJV)*

Again, He did it! He laid the foundation of the household of God. He is the chief corner stone. He founded His Church upon the foundation of His own sacrifice.

> *"In whom all the building fitly framed together groweth into a holy temple in the Lord: In whom ye also are builded together for a habitation of God **through the Spirit**."*
>
> 2:21-22(KJV)

He did it! He is doing it if we will just let Him. He wants to grow us into a holy temple, a dwelling place of God. That is the purpose of this dispensation – to grow the Church into His habitation, the "place" where He lives from generation to generation. **And it is by the Spirit!** By the Spirit the Church will be this habitation and by no other way.

I don't know if I'm seeing something that isn't there or am not seeing something that is there but the essence of what Christ gave us was to live as His Church and He would change the world. We are just told to go into the world and be who He has made us and He will change it. In other words, the world will be different just because we are in it. The world was to be different just because Israel walked through it not because they were to do something – they were simply to be His. We can't do anything but be His.

Why is this so difficult?

Human beings love to be in control because it is safe. One of the thrills of being on a roller coaster is to get just a little bit of the feeling of being out of control. We still see the tracks and the people getting off safely who rode before us. We know what to expect. But to yield completely to the Holy Spirit means that we never know what will be next and that terrifies us. We say, "Why not just do what we think God would do and leave well enough alone?" This has most often been our creed but it is disobedience.

> *"For to be carnally minded is death but to be spiritually minded is life and peace. Because the carnal mind is enmity against God: for it is not subject to the law of God neither can it be."*
> *Romans 8:6-7(KJV)*

Our plans and purposes, what comes out of our minds, is enmity against God. The word *law* in verse 7 is a *distributing* or an *assigning* or in other words, God gives us or assigns us what we are to think and do. He does this through the Holy Spirit who lives within us and is the access which we have to the Father. The carnal mind cannot hear God because it is set apart from hearing Him, it is at odds with Him and verse 6 says that *"to be carnally minded is death."*

> *"But the natural man receiveth not the things of the Spirit of God: for they are foolishness unto Him: neither can he know them, because they are spiritually discerned. But he that is spiritual judgeth all things, yet he himself is judged of no man."*
> *I Corinthians 2:14(KJV)*

The *natural man* is the one who is governed only by his senses and discerns only what he can see, hear, feel, taste and smell. The Church has been carnal, making decisions based on sensual knowledge rather than the revelation of the Holy Spirit.

The most important words that you and I could ever read and understand regarding our subject are these: **"So then they that are in the flesh cannot please God."** Romans 8:8 (KJV)

Practical Aspects

If I have put forth the truth and it is the Holy Spirit that speaks to and guides and directs Christians to really be the people of God then what is the "formula" for walking by the Spirit? How are we to live this spiritual life?

> *"But ye are not in the flesh, but in the Spirit, if so be that the Spirit of God dwell in you. Now if any man have not the Sprit of Christ, he is none of His."*
> *Romans 8:9(KJV)*

We must operate as the people of God, led by His Spirit and must be separate from those who have never been filled or who deny the Spirit's leadership. We cannot peacefully co-exist with those that do not believe; those who are carnally minded. This is not because we don't love them and minister to them, but they must not have a say in where the Church is being led.

We must put to death the flesh in our corporate existence. *"For if ye live after the flesh, ye shall die: but if ye through the Spirit do mortify the deeds of the body, ye shall live." Romans 8:13(KJV)*

We must live and give life. The world needs the influence of Christ and only by the work of the Spirit through us will we communicate that life to the earth. The entire nation of Israel had to be obedient to God's direction concerning the Passover in order to come out of Egypt to be God's people. We must do the same. We have a religious system that has made anyone who darkens the door of the Church regularly a member with full rights and privileges. The system must be radically changed to only include in the revelation of God to the Church those who can hear Him.

"For as many as are led by the Spirit of God, they are the sons of God."
Romans 8:14(KJV)

Each of you reading this will have to decide for yourself exactly how this can happen in your fellowship. You might need to tighten up the membership rules that allow those that do not show true repentance and lifestyle change and who do not openly proclaim Christ from having a say. But my personal opinion is that there should not be church membership or any of the other non-biblical, cultural idiosyncrasies that we have invented. We need to get back to the pure message of Scripture to determine what we are and where He wants to take us. We need to examine the Word to find the places we have ignored the truth and formed our own contraptions that do not communicate Christ to the earth.

Chapter 9

Misplaced Gifts

Probably the greatest tragedy in our broken religious system is the neglect of the gifts that God gives to His people to further His kingdom work.

> *"And he gave some, apostles; and some, prophets; and some, evangelists; and some, pastors and teachers; for the perfecting of the saints for the work of the ministry, for the edifying of the body of Christ.*
>
> *Ephesians 4:11-12(KJV)*

These "gift ministries" as I will refer to them, have been mistakenly defined, ignored or even denied in our denominational life. In order for the Word of God to course through this world, affecting cultures and societies, there must be an adherence to the Godly order and obedience to the divine design. God would never institute a ministry for no reason; they are designed to fill absolute needs absolutely. The church, over the centuries, has defined the roles of these ministries and combined functions without regard for the truth. Where are the apostles? Evangelists? Prophets?

Christianity still recognizes pastors and teachers but have changed the role to where it is barely discernable as the biblical servant of the people. A look at each of these roles from a biblical perspective is in order and I will present them to you simply and succinctly the way the Word of God does.

Apostles

Much of the confusion that we see in our doctrine regarding the apostolic ministry is the difference between the Apostles (capital A) and apostles (small a). The original twelve were Apostles and are the prototype of all that would come later. The word is *"apostolos"* and literally means one who has been *"sent"* or an *"ambassador."* In a very real sense, it is necessary to understand that nowhere in scripture is the church told to ordain apostles but the job description still exists. *"It was he who gave some to be apostles, some to be prophets, some to be evangelists, and some to be pastors and teachers, to prepare God's people for works of service, so that the body of Christ may be built up ... "*

We need to deal with the fact that *Ephesians 4:11* is written to the church, does not refer to the original twelve and fills a very practical need in the church today. Not everyone on this earth has heard the gospel of Christ nor has the entire world even heard the name of Christ. Our verse gives the gift ministries to the Church and *verse 13* says that it is *"until we all come in the unity of the faith, and of the knowledge of the Son of God, unto a perfect man, unto the measure of the stature of the fullness of Christ." (KJV)* That has not happened yet! Why are we so bent on denying so many of the things that God has given us to reach the world including gifted ministers?

The apostle in our day and time would be roughly what we would call a missionary; true Godly ordained missionaries that tell people who have never heard the name "Jesus" about the One who gave His life for them. Having served on the board of directors of the largest mission sending organization in the world, I can personally tell you that not all of the people that we term missionaries are included in our definition of apostle. Many support personal are in the field not to personally proclaim the gospel but to support others who do. There is also the element of church planting to the apostolic ministry. The natural outgrowth of telling people about Christ is having them respond to Christ. They need to be taught how to come together in worship and in order. The role of the apostle is not to do this on a permanent basis but is to set it up so that the church has its leadership. Paul filled every one of these roles and is the ideal. He is the defining example of the apostolic ministry and neither the church nor the world has changed enough to change the role.

I have a friend in Tanzania, an African, who is pastor of an indigenous church that prays for Gods' leading as to which tribe to go to as so many of them are un-reached. His church identifies a group, an area and then prays for the methods. He goes and lives with them for a time until Christ is established in their lives. He continues to be connected by rising up local leadership and keeping in contact with them, returning periodically to see how they are doing and to teach them.

In the American church culture, we can call church planters, true church planters, apostles. They go from place to place, witnessing Christ, establishing fellowships, raising up local leadership and then moving on. Like Paul, they have a lifelong attachment to the churches that they have started and stay in relationship by returning to preach and teach. They do not pastor as pastoring is not their call. They are apostles – church planters.

The problem that we find in western church life is that everyone who has a call to full time ministry is called a pastor. We plug everyone into a mold that for the most part, they do not fit. This is especially true regarding evangelists.

Evangelists

There is a gifted minister that God has given to the church called an evangelist or the Greek *"euaggelistes."* This word means *"one who declares the good news"* but is distinguished more by whom he declares the "good news" to. An evangelist will go to the most obvious of the lost, the dregs of society that it takes some getting dirty to reach. Now please understand that I am not speaking necessarily about economic standing but more about spiritual standing. There can be just as much evangelistic need on Wall St. as on Main St. He or she will go to the places that are frequented by the lost, bringing them to Christ and pointing them toward the people who can disciple them. They do not do the discipling themselves but make sure that it is taken care of because there are many others that they are being called to reach. Understand that we are not talking about a fellow in a powder blue suit that rents an arena and preaches a series of messages but someone who invests enough of their life into a person or a few people to bring them to the Lord.

The biblical example of what we are talking about is Philip in *Acts 8:26-40*, who at the bidding of the Holy Spirit goes in the opposite direction that is natural and speaks to one person. That person may be influential like the Ethiopian eunuch or may be a "nobody," it matters only to God. The return is not the important thing but rather obedience to the revelation of the Holy Spirit. Again, we put the function of an evangelist on what we call the pastor because we deny their reality and their importance.

Prophets

Out of the three gift ministries that the modern church denies or distorts, apostle, evangelist and prophet, the one that is the most controversial is the prophet. In most fellowships, if someone stands up before the people and speaks a word from the Lord, he or she will probably be asked to leave. The prophet looks the body square in the eye and says, *"Thus saith the Lord!"* The message can be one of judgment, condemnation or even blessing but the problem is that the words come when the church needs them and not necessarily when they want them. It usually addresses a glaring sin or need. The prophet must be recognized as a gift from God for the edification of the body or we will get rid of every one of them in order to not have to live with their message. There must be integrity in our corporate existence or the prophet will meet the same fate that they did in the Old Testament; either death to the prophet himself or at least the death of his message.

The "broken cistern" that we have built will not hold this gift. Prophecy is too confrontational and is designed by God to bring conviction and convincing, neither of which sit well with modern congregations. There are too many other "churches" to go to if toes begin being stepped on. Pastors feel that the people must be protected from conviction that leads to repentance or there will be a mass exodus, a depletion of funds and personal accountability before the powers that be. The only power that should be is a Holy and Righteous God and the prophet should be welcomed. The church should expect them and nurture them holding them accountable but free to operate in their ministry.

A church that I recently pastored had a man whom God had sent to us with an obvious prophetic gift. I supported him, even though he was a little rough around the edges I really sought to get the people to listen to what he said as being the Word of God. I tried to get them to weigh what he said against what the Word said and to recognize that these were areas in which God was trying to get our attention. There was so much controversy and rejection of his gift that I was asked to leave because of my support for his message.

Pastor/Teacher

This is the category that all of the anointed, called men and women of God are lumped into if they show any bent toward Christian service. If you walk to the front of any church in America with a call to ministry, everyone will automatically assume that you will one day be a pastor/teacher. This is the poor fellow who "leads the church," that is the CEO, building contractor, healer, visitor, social director and any other role that the congregation decides they are paying him for.

In truth, he is the one that is gifted in teaching the Word of God and discipling the people in the proper living out of the Word. His or her heart is always on seeing the people abound in His grace and love and growing in a love for God. There is no way to do this other than by investing ones' life in others' lives and this call is to stay where the people are. It will never be a stepping stone to something else but is an end in itself. It is not a job but a call and God is the final authority on when this ministry is over in an area and it can be assumed that that end is death.

There is also the element of protection from danger. The pastor/teacher is to protect the flock of God from ravenous wolves who seek to devour the people of God spiritually, keeping them from being productive for the kingdom. Not only is protection given from immediate danger but also that the assembly would be sharp to the methods of the enemy for safety in the future.

This pastoral ministry is not what we are now seeing in our church structure because the way we have defined him is having all the roles of all the gift ministries. We have to start seeing the complete church having apostles, prophets, evangelists and pastor teachers. If not, we will remain barren and unproductive having minimal effect on a dying world.

But what is the context in which these ministries are supposed to function? The answer is the city wide church. When an apostle is called by God, he should be sent out by the church in his city to the area in which the city feels a corporate leaning. In Charleston, West Virginia there seems to be a connection with East and Central Africa. We have contacts with church planters there and if we have someone who shows a call to church planting then we have a natural field of ministry in West Virginia, the United States and East Africa. Of course God could change that but it is nice to know that there is a pattern of heartfelt desire for the needs of a particular area. Our small fellowship has a personal call to Haiti and Belarus that comes from past contacts and ministry and God seems to have given us a heart for these places.

> *"Now there were in the church"* (the city wide church) *that was at Antioch certain prophets and teachers; as Barnabas, and Simeon that was called Niger, and Lucius of Cyrene, and Manaen, which had been brought up with Herod the tetrarch, and Saul."*
>
> *"As they ministered to the Lord, and fasted, the Holy Ghost said, 'Separate me Barnabas and Saul for the work whereunto I have called them."*
>
> *"And when they had fasted and prayed, and laid their hands on them, they sent them away."*
> Acts 13:1-3(KJV)

The Church in the city of Antioch, all of the believers, was responsible for sending out Paul and Barnabas under the direction of the Holy Spirit. There was no mission organization, simply the church in a city recognizing the call on men's lives and praying for guidance in how those gifts should be utilized. *"They sent them away!"* They were basking under the *"fountain of living waters,"* the cisterns had not yet been built. There were no denominations! There were still apostles, prophets and teachers and Philip had already been called as the prototype evangelist. The gifts were functioning!

Organism As Opposed To Organization

This would be a good place to interject the idea of the difference between an organism and an organization. In everything that God is responsible for, there is life. Jesus said, *"I have come that you might have life and you might have it more abundantly."* John 10:10b The Greek word for *"life"* is *"zoe"* which means *"life and all that God intended life to be."* When we look at God's ideal for life, we are confronted by the Garden of Eden where God and man were in perfect fellowship, man had no fear and there were no needs. There was life in all of its fullness – this is God's intent.

The *"zoe"* life of the Garden was reestablished for us spiritually at our new birth but not physically. Spiritually we are to live in completeness and the greatness of living in Christ is to be communicated to the world. This is organism. Living life and showing God's glory is organism. **Organism** is living under the "fountain of living waters."

Organization is just the opposite. It is making the best of brokenness and living without relationship. It is seeking to please God from effort rather than heart and can only result in frustration and death. It is the way of Cain. In the incredible novel *"East of Eden"* by John Steinbeck, we have the story of two sons who both have a love for their father but ones' love is for the right reasons and the other's isn't. You see we can love God for what He can do for us. It feels good to us to love and be loved but that must never be the reason. Love must always be for the others benefit. It must always seek to please the one being loved. Anything else comes more from a love for self rather than a love for others. This is religion.

Religion, the efforts of man to please God, results in organization. Business. Hierarchy. Lowerarchy.

Organism and organization are the difference between life and death, good and evil, fountains and cisterns. It is absolutely imperative that the church come out of what is called Christianity and become the living organism that Christ died for and the Holy Spirit came to lead. In organism, the gifts will abound and lives will be changed.

In *Ephesians 4:12*, which follows up the presentation of the gift ministries, we have the reason for these ministers.

> *"...for the perfecting of the saints for the work of the ministry, for the edifying of the body of Christ."*

Apostles, prophets, evangelists and pastor/teachers are to equip each of the believers in the church to do the work of the ministry or even better put in the context of the Word, that all will do the work that results from the love of God that lives in their hearts and overflows in their lives. There is a corporate aspect to organism also. We have already established the fact that God never intended Christians to live in personal isolation but to function as a unit, a living being. Organisms have different parts and draw their strength and life from the fact that they are complete.

How long are we intended to be this living, breathing, efficacious force on the earth?

> *"Till we all come in the unity of the faith, and the knowledge of God, unto a perfect man, unto*

> *the measure of the stature of the fullness of Christ:*
> *that we henceforth be no more children tossed to and fro, and carried about with every wind of doctrine, by the sleight of men, and cunning craftiness, whereby they lie in wait to deceive;*
> *but speaking the truth in love, may grow up into him in all things, which is the head, even Christ:*
> *from whom the whole body fitly joined together and compacted by that which every joint supplieth, according to the effectual working in the measure of every part, maketh increase of the body unto the edifying of itself in love."*
> Ephesians 4:13-16(KJV)

The process of our perfection as the body of Christ began at Pentecost and will continue until we are presented as a spotless bride before the Father by the Son. Until that time, we are to cooperate with our Lord in our edification, our building up, our transformation into fullness in Christ.

The gift ministries are essential in order for us to grow up *"unto a perfect man, unto the measure of the stature of the fullness of Christ."*

Our broken cisterns have caused the ministries that are at the heart of our growth to be rejected, distorted or ignored.

Chapter 10

Ministries for Everyone

In the book of *Romans*, in chapter 12, Paul gives one of the most powerful doctrinal statements as to God's methods of building the city church.

> "I beseech you therefore, brethren, by the mercies of God, that ye present your bodies a living sacrifice, holy, acceptable unto God, which is your reasonable service."
>
> *(v1) (KJV)*

The church is told that when Christ redeems us, we respond with the offering of our life. We give Him back what He has given as an offering. No longer is a dead sacrifice, a lamb or a goat or a turtledove necessary to please God but since He has given the perfect sacrifice we offer our lives.

"And be not conformed to this world but be ye transformed by the renewing of your mind, that ye may prove what is that good and acceptable and perfect will of God." *(v2) (KJV)* Our life is given to be transformed by God, changed in nature by Him, and then presented back to Him as an offering.

A caterpillar is changed into a butterfly not by its own effort but by the perfect design of God. It must get itself to the place on the tree where it can attach itself in order for God to do what He does. There is effort on our part needed for God to be able to do His part. When we are where He needs us to be, He transforms us.

This transformation is not in our spiritual nature, as that has already been changed through our faith in Christ, but is in the process of sanctification that all believers must go through that we may continually grow to live more and more outwardly what we really are inwardly.

The next verse in the 12th chapter of *Romans* is often ignored in its context but when understood gives new light to the whole chapter.

> *"For I say, through the grace given unto me, to every man that is among you, not to think of himself more highly than he ought to think; but to think soberly, according as God has dealt to every man the measure of faith."*
>
> *(v3) (KJV)*

A Christian is not to *"think of himself more highly than he ought to think"* because it goes against the corporate, organic nature of the church! We are not to function individually but in harmony with all others. Your gifts have no use by themselves but must be in concert with everyone else's gifts in order to function properly. What do many believers say as soon as their gifts begin to become obvious? "I've got to go where I can exercise my gift." The mistake is in the fact that God gave that gift to function in that believer because it was needed where he or she is! The problem is that our broken cistern has taught us to look to our own fulfillment rather than the development of the true church.

> *"For as we have many members in one body, and all the members have not the same office: So we being many are one body in Christ, and every one members of one another."*
>
> *(v4-5) (KJV)*

Interaction between the gifts is the sign of life in the body of Christ. Jesus allowed the people around Him to function in their anointing and their call. He understood that He was building a body. He was able to lead them in the way of organic unity rather than allow them to go the way of fragmented, self centered division. Remember that God's goal is to build the people of God not the persons of God. He is able to take each person in the way He has made them and plug them in exactly where they belong in the church. It is His responsibility.

The Motivational Gifts

Each Christian has inherent within himself a "heart" for ministry. It is what motivates him and governs how one sees the needs of the world around him. It is not the gift itself but what energizes it. It is essential that church leadership recognize and understand these motivations. Paul did this and addressed them in the latter portion of *Romans 12*.

The nature of our religious system has been for one person, the pastor, or in larger churches the paid staff, to do all of the work of ministry. This arrangement has contributed to the main body of believers being passive and stagnant, letting the gifts of God within them waste away. Within everyone who names Jesus as Lord there is a call to touch others with the love of Christ but with each person that touch is coming from a different place inside. In *Romans 12:6-8*, Paul is describing those different attitudes of ministry of the people of the church.

"We have different gifts, according to the grace given us. If a man's gift is prophesying, let him use it in proportion to his faith. If it is serving, let him serve; if it is teaching, let him teach; if it is encouraging, let him encourage; if it is contributing to the needs of others, let him give generously; if it is leadership, let him govern diligently; if it is showing mercy. Let him do it cheerfully."
(v6-8)

People who God has given a prophetic gift will see everything in either black or white and will look at everything in front of them as being sin or righteousness. They will want to know whether others understand what God says about what they are doing and if there is sin in the camp they will vociferously point it out. The down side to people with this bent is the fact that they can have a tendency to reject the other gifts because theirs is so absolute. This must be dealt with in love and respect.

The one with the gift of service however, is always looking towards the needs of others, always asking, "How can I help?" Here too there can be a down side in that servers sometimes relegate the vocal gifts, preaching and teaching, to a lesser level. It is difficult for the servant to do nothing even when nothing is what is called for. There is such a depth of compassion to those with the gift of service.

One of the most obvious of the motivational gifts is that of teacher. We tend to look at this individual as being the one in the church who has the call other than the pastor. Sunday school teachers, Bible study teachers and the pastor are what we think of here but we are missing the attitude present in one who sees things from a theological perspective. Everything is evaluated from a desire to see the people learn and understand. "What section of scripture addresses this issue?" is their first response in looking at any question.

Pride can enter into this person's heart and a desire for self glorification. The teacher doesn't give general messages but very profound, direct truth, pointed first at the local fellowship and then at the city-wide Church.

The gift of exhortation speaks encouragement to all who need it. The body of Christ is built up by this person in ways that are essential. The Greek word means *"to call to ones' side"* which gives us the picture of comfort and an instilling of confidence in another. What would the church be without these comforters? The thing that must be guarded against by the one who exhorts is an unwillingness to confront sin.

Where would we be without leaders? In the broken cisterns of today's church, all of the leadership falls either on the person that we call the pastor or the "powerful" people of the church. In either case the role is distorted to indicate that decisions are made by the leader. Contrast this with Jesus who was the perfect leader and His main purpose was in showing by example how to be a follower. He said, *"I tell you the truth, the Son can do nothing by himself; he can only do what he sees his Father doing, because whatever the Father does the Son also does." John 5:19* Jesus was a follower and "followership" is a quality that is not propagated under our religious system. Only followers can truly lead especially in Christ's church. The negative tendency in a person with leadership and administration gifts is to be autocratic, to think that it is their way or the highway.

The last of the motivational gifts of *Romans 12* is "showing mercy" which is the person who finds the brother or sister who is hurting and touches them to ease the hurt. They thrive on touch as opposed to the exhorter who thrives on ministry with words. The mercy giver is the one who doesn't need to say anything. Long before Jesus cried, *"Father forgive them for they know not what they do,"* Jesus was showing mercy. He was able to speak to the thief on the cross words of love, forgiveness and compassion even in the midst of His horrible pain. Due to the lean to emotion in this gift, there is a tendency to forget Bible truth because of the intense feelings that are aroused.

Does our religious scheme make use of the motivational gifts that God has placed in His people? Are these gifts lost in the scattered church life of today? I believe that the logical conclusion must be that this is true. The gifts of most of the people in the pews are neither recognized nor nurtured. All of these abilities must be all mixed together, energized by the Holy Spirit and allowed to be lived out in the life of the body and when they are the world will be different.

Think about an army in the heat of battle, having all of the artillery ever invented, superior troop strength, air support and everything else necessary to fight a war and win but refusing to use it. Instead the Generals, Colonels, Majors and Captains pick up the arms and go out to the battlefield, leaving the troops and sophisticated weapons behind. This is what the church has chosen as a method of operation. The paid leadership are the ones on the front lines while the real soldiers, the ones charged with fighting the war, are simply waiting for reports from the front.

Most of the wonderful Christians who have been paid for by Jesus would love to be taught how to fight the battle. They want to know what they have been called to and look for a true Church that will receive and help them develop their gift. The only problem is that the clergy might work themselves out of a job if the people really were taught what Christ wants to do through them. If the Church really understood the power that was in each individual Christian it would be different, much different. Picture believers walking down streets, asking the sick whether they want to be healed; ministering in Christ's name, seeing God given the glory He deserves.

The Manifestations

When a person confesses Jesus as Lord an incredible regeneration takes place.

"As for you, you were dead in your transgressions and sins..." Ephesians 2:1 A human being who was born into spiritual death because of the sin of distant forefathers is made alive through faith in the payment of Jesus Christ for that sin. Much of Christianity understands this truth but fails to recognize something else that happens because of what Jesus did. We become filled with the Holy Spirit!

> *"If you love me, you will obey what I command. And I will ask the Father, and he will give you another Counselor to be with you forever – the Spirit of truth. The world cannot accept him, because it neither sees him or knows him. But you know him, for he lives with you and will be in you."*
>
> *John 14:15-17*

Jesus stated that at a time in the future the Holy Spirit will not just be with you but will be in you. This came to pass later at the day of Pentecost and *"and all of them were **filled** with the Holy Spirit..."* Acts 2:4a

> *"Then Peter, **filled** with the Holy Spirit, said to them..."*
>
> *Acts 4:8*
>
> *"After they prayed, the place where they were meeting was shaken. And they were all **filled** with the Holy Spirit and spoke the word boldly."*
>
> *Acts 4:31*
>
> *"Then Saul, who was also called Paul, **filled***

> with the Holy Spirit, looked strait at Elymas and said..."
>
> Acts 13:9

In these verses, there is the clear indication that the Greek word, *"pletho"*, *"filled"*, has associated with it an action. Something happens when people are filled to overflowing with the Holy Spirit. The world sees and this is the manifestation of the Spirit that I Corinthians talks about when it says, *"... now to each one the **manifestation** of the Spirit is given for the common good."* Acts 12:7 A manifestation is an outward show of an inner reality.

The manifestations are different from the "gift ministries" and the "motivational gifts" that we have already looked at. The manifestations of the Spirit are the results of the Holy Spirit indwelling the people of God and are seen as these nine different, interdependent ways:

"the message of wisdom"
"the message of knowledgse"
"faith"
"gifts of healing"
"miraculous powers"
"prophecy"
"distinguishing between spirits"
"speaking in different kinds of tongues"
"the interpretation of tongues"

All nine ways in which the Holy Spirit is made known in the life of the Christian should regularly be seen in the life of the church depending on what is needed. They are given for *"the common good"* and until we are in glory they will be needed by the body. Most of mainline Christianity refuses to talk about **revelation** (wisdom, knowledge and discerning of spirits), **impartation** (tongues, interpretation of tongues and prophecy) and **demonstration** (faith, miracles and healings). Many of us have been fully lied to by those who said that these manifestations passed away with the disciples, or who say that they are demonic or who say that they still exist but we don't need them.

Think logically! Why would God make available to us things that are useless? Why would He allow the people that He loves and cherishes to be fooled? Why would He end the manifestations that so powerfully showed His presence so soon and for no apparent reason?

What our broken religious system, our broken cistern has done is decide "truth" and then set out to prove it. Whenever a Bible student already has his or her mind made up and then goes to Scripture, there is no doubt that they will prove their notion. But to bask under the fountain of living waters it is imperative that we believe and live the truth even if it goes against what we already believe.

We have built a whole religious structure by picking and choosing the gifts of God like we are in a buffet line. *"I'll take that, that and a little bit of that. I don't like that or that. I want a lot of that."* Poor, innocent, Christians have bought into this without knowing, without being taught. Even though I spoke in tongues the night I was saved, not knowing anything about it, alone in my home, as the result of a prayer that said *"whatever you have Lord, I want it,"* I soon found that what I was so excited about was not welcome at most gatherings of Christians. I didn't understand. I did it! I was given it by the Father who had just saved me

In order to pastor the Baptist church that God had called me to I was told that I would have to *"stop doing that."* I did for four years and it was like four years of barely being able to breathe. When my Spirit would long to tell God the depths of my heart, I had to try for English words that would say what I thought was inside. Ridiculous! Not only was I not allowed to teach people the whole gospel, but I was forbidden to pray to God in a way that I had been doing for sixteen years. I really felt that this church was where I was supposed to be so I stayed faithful to the call to keep my mouth shut about tongues. What kind of system ignores and denies the truth?

If we are to ever be the spiritual presence that God has intended, we will need to get rid of fear and bigotry and not hold God or His gifts responsible for the actions of people who abuse them.

Wouldn't you think that every Christian would start from an honest question about what these manifestations are? Instead, we deny them, forbid them and allow them to divide us. Wouldn't you think that it would please God if we at least said, *"I don't understand. I want all He has but I just don't understand."*

We teach tithing in most Christian churches in the world but it is mentioned in the New Testament eight times, all referring to Israel and when addressed by Jesus, spoken of from a negative perspective. We ignore similar laws in the Old Testament on the Sabbath and claim that Jesus has freed us from the consequences of disobeying the dictates of the law. Yet the manifestation of tongues, the "bone of contention" for most of the church is mentioned twenty five times and when everything is taken in context there is not one negative. For some reason our system, cistern, has decided that tithing is good and tongues are bad.

Unless we are able to take all the gifts that people have as a result of the Spirit living within them, and allow them to function and interact, we will never see revival. We can cry out for the Spirit to come when He has already come and we have told Him to leave. We should simply look at the truth of the Word, with no preconceived notions and live in the fullness of His gift. We can pray for the Holy Spirit to overflow in us as the manifestations, giving us credibility in the world or we can continue to deny them and experience very little results.

The church must choose.

Chapter 11

The Path

Close your eyes and picture an opening into a forest. It is a clearly defined place to enter into a beautiful virgin stand of trees. It is obvious that there is a path and that many have entered at this place before. The forest is beautiful! Large trees perfectly spaced to let shafts of sunlight beam throughout. There is very little undergrowth and an almost grassy like floor is everywhere with a fern here and there and other soft growth. You walk along so peaceful and secure that you hardly notice the subtle changes. The undergrowth gets just a little thicker and the path gets just a little bit less defined. The changes are barely noticeable so your demeanor doesn't change and your thoughts go on to other things. At any time you can decide to turn and go back but you don't see the need.

More and more the trees encroach onto the trail and it even becomes necessary to step around a tree every once in a while. The path has more growth on it and some of that growth is hard, with thorns and weedy plants. As you look to the sides you notice that there is no longer that soft grassy floor to the forest and the brush is thicker – no ferns or soft plants here. It is still not too late to turn back but you think that there is just too much invested to abandon your way now. Going along it occurs to you to look behind and it is very difficult to see where you have come from. Everything is getting thicker and it is more obvious every minute that you are getting lost. It is too late to turn back now. You are lost and beginning to panic.

With every step, the hope of finding the way out gets less likely and the thorns are beginning to tear your clothes and your skin and your hope. You stand in the middle of this mess dejected and afraid.

The only thing to do is to cry out; to scream for help. Scream loud so someone, anyone might hear. Anyone would look good right now. He hears, Jesus hears, almost as soon as the Words come out of you mouth, there He stands. As is His character, He reaches out to you; the look on His face is one of comfort, safety and deliverance and you wonder why you didn't realize and cry out sooner.

This point is critical because what Jesus wants you to understand is that you are on the wrong path. He doesn't want to make things right where you are but wants to lead you out so that you can start over again on the right trail. When He takes you there you see that it looks remarkably like the first path at its start but as you go along you realize that this one never changes. It is consistent and doesn't deviate and gradually proves that it is the way of blessing and wonder. It is sure and certain.

This analogy speaks of the journey all of us are going through as followers of Jesus Christ. He had to take each of us out of the mess that we had made of our lives and bring us to a new path of forgiveness and righteousness. The church of Jesus Christ has not gotten to this point yet and is still wandering around thinking that she can find her way out. The Lord extends His hand and beckons for her to take it; take it to be led out of the mess she finds herself in. Stubbornness has yet to allow her to be led out and directed to the second entrance to the true path. The church cries, *"Fix me where I am, I want to stay here and have you change my circumstances."* Jesus says, *"You must follow me to the right way.*

He has given us His Word which is the truth; He has given us Himself, the Word in the flesh. The Father called His servant Israel in the book of Jeremiah and in all of the prophetic books to come back to Him. The church must come back to Him, not just in word but in deed.

There is a pastors group in our city that has been meeting together for years in prayer and fellowship, mission trips and joint worship. I sought this communion with these leaders of Christ's church with all of my heart and am very happy to see the beginnings of unity in the area. However, I don't believe that we will see the outpouring of the glory of God until we are willing to completely be one. After our meetings we go back into our fragmented, broken cistern. Our heart says unity and our hearts want unity but we don't realize that we are not coming out of what has caused us to be divided in the first place. The black churches and the white churches are beginning to get together but they are still black churches and white churches. We love each other but are resigned to the fact that we can't live together longer than a couple of hours. The Pentecostals and the liturgical churches find it fascinating to share a service here and there but they aren't willing to *"submit to one another out of reverence for Christ."* Like the path that leads nowhere, we are not willing for Him to lead us deciding rather to stay where we are and have Him deal with us there. He won't. He can't.

The old self built system, cistern, needs to go. It needs to be torn down and we need to return to the "fountain of living waters." How can we possibly get rid of something that has meant so much to us? How can we give up our tradition and our heritage? The decision needs to be made as to whether we care more about our traditions than we do about obedience. We must decide whether we will maintain our broken cisterns or bask under the fountain of living waters.

Whenever people find themselves deep in turmoil and confusion there is the tendency to want to give up. The predicament that Christ's Bride finds herself in may seem impossible to untangle. The Word of God, however, gives us clear direction as to how to live like a *"... a chosen people, a royal priesthood, a holy nation, a people belonging to God, that you may declare the praise of him who called you out of darkness into his wonderful light." I Peter 2:9* In the context of this verse the church is told about submitting to the authorities in the world, summed up in the verse 17, *"Show proper respect to everyone: Love the brotherhood of believers, fear God, honor the king."*

"Love the brotherhood of believers, fear God, honor the king," brings to mind the beautiful truth of *Acts 2:47* which says that the believers were, *"praising God and enjoying the favor of all the people. And the Lord added to their number daily those who were being saved."*

How can we get back to the purity of faith and fellowship of those early days in order to see the same conditions result? The answer is unequivocally that we must get rid of the things that changed the church. What came into Christianity that robbed the body of Christ of the simplicity of their first love?

Buildings

The obvious representations of the church in our world today are the buildings that we call "churches." Just as a house does not make a home, a building does not make a church. Speaking matter of factly, let me say that the buildings that we find so necessary are actually one of the biggest reasons for the church being an organization rather than an organism. They are the most obvious way for Satan to sneak into our fellowship. The maintenance of what we have built actually turns us into corporations rather than gatherings of Christians. In our system, we allow people to come off the streets and be part of our fellowship, never having professed faith and Lordship in Christ, never showing the fruit of Christian love just because they show abilities that the church feels are needed. We think we need people who can manage money, take on major building projects or who have the money to donate to these projects. Never mind that relationship with God through Christ has never been experienced. Of course we should love these people and welcome them into our groups but we shouldn't give them control and leadership over property and money. We vote unbelievers onto boards and committees that are determining what the body of Christ can and can't do. Paul told the church at Corinth:

> *"Do not be yoked together with unbelievers. For what do righteousness and wickedness have in common? Or what fellowship can light have with darkness? What harmony is there between Christ and Belial? What does a believer have in common with an unbeliever?*
>
> *2 Corinthians 6:14-15*

If you have been around Christianity any length of time you will probably be able to identify with the facts above. You have seen belief in Christ and unbelief attempt to peacefully co-exist with devastating results. Most of these results are in the realm of earthly endeavors rather than the pursuit of true spirituality; questions over what color the carpet should be rather than what the Holy Spirit is saying. Buildings that have been mistaken for the church are wide open invitations for the devil and his troops to have free reign in Christianity.

We think that if we build enough then we can attract people rather than allowing the Holy Spirit to lead the lost to our fellowship to be changed. Our hearts tell us that if we can only have more to offer than the church down the street then we will have visitors that we can tell about Jesus. This leads to people becoming part of our bodies that have never experienced true repentance and bring all the problems of the world into the congregation. They get elected to positions of responsibility because of their talents and finances without evidence of true relationship with Christ.

Our decisions as the redeemed body of the Lord should never be affected by those who don't know Christ. Where the Holy Spirit is leading the church to minister cannot be discerned by those who aren't filled with the Spirit. Yet by our nature, the church allows anyone who wants to be part of the gathering of saints to be there and even have a governing say.

What if the church was simply a coming together of Christians for the Lord's Supper, teaching and singing and hearing from God? Who, other than believers or those who are truly being drawn to Christ, would want to come to a meeting like this? What if there were no gymnasiums or bus trips, no Valentines parties or Christmas programs? The church would come together wherever there was an empty office or store or even at people's homes; they would be like a real family with nothing but faith in Christ to hold them together. Picture a body that meets because the people love each other rather than that it is good for business or "it's just what you do on Sunday." I know that this is not true of every church that has a building but if you have decided that the broken cistern is not what you want then you must know that there are alternatives. There are schools, hotels, museums, community centers and many other buildings that are vacant on Sundays and are available to the church. You get rejuvenated, you show your love for God and your brothers and sisters and then you go back out into the world, speaking the good news of Jesus Christ. Think of the leadership of the church doing nothing but teaching the pure Word in love and the truth doing its work; peoples' lives being transformed by its power.

You will often hear believers say, "The church is not a building it's the people." They say it but they don't mean it. We operate as if it was the building and if you want to be part of the church then you need to come to the building. If you ask very many Christians whether someone is a Christian or not you will probably hear, *"He doesn't go to church."* It has nothing to do with going anywhere but in being something.

If you are dying in the broken cistern then come out; come out of the pile of bricks and mortar and be the *"whole building joined together."* If you are thriving then stay but if your heart longs for something different then come out. I once asked a dear pastor friend of mine if he thought that you could develop the true church within the context of the traditional church. He told me that he didn't think so. I thought for a minute and told him that I had to try. Within two years the church that I was in asked me to leave because I was taking them where they didn't want to go. I was trying to take them away from being a building where people meet to people whom the world wants to meet. I wanted to see all of the people have a chance to participate in what we were and see their gifts developed and to have the opportunity to express themselves. The rebellion against anything out of the ordinary was obvious and I could feel the polarization in the church increasing each week. It was impossible for two mindsets to exist in the church because we are told in Philippians 2:2 *"to be like-minded, having the same love, being one in spirit and purpose. Do nothing out of selfish ambition but in humility consider others better than yourselves."* If we are unable to live our corporate lives in the same mind and the same love and putting each other ahead of ourselves then we are probably not all believers and will never communicate Christ to the nations.

In most churches that are experiencing division, the biggest fight is over who gets the building. *"Are you going to leave or are we going to leave." "This is my church and I'm not leaving!"* What they mean is that in this "divorce," who will wind up with the property. Only in a false system would material things cause strife and schism in people whose unity cost God His only Son. It is the system that is flawed and the real body of Christ needs to come out of it. Satan loves our religion and loves it to be furthered. We play into his hands and give up the freedom of walking in the Spirit in favor of walking in the jurisdiction of the one who would *"steal, kill and destroy"* and by doing so, the earth is denied the deliverance that the church has been charged with conveying.

Are these piles of bricks and mortar so important that we are willing to sacrifice our focus on Him and His kingdom? Are our buildings really necessary in order for there to be a presence of the church in our cities? When the church was at its most powerful and effective was a time when they had nothing but love and community and were not grouped according to the place they worshipped but by who they worshipped. Did things need to change? I think not.

Professional Clergy

> *"But if the watchman sees the sword coming and does not blow the trumpet to warn the people and the sword comes and takes the life of one of them, that man shall be taken away because of his sin,*

> *but I will hold the watchman accountable for his blood."*
>
> Ezekiel 33:6

The word of the Lord came to Ezekiel telling him to speak to his country, Israel, and tell them that judgment was coming. God told him emphatically that his responsibility was in making the proclamation not in whether the people were obedient. He made it clear that if the call was sounded but not obeyed then it would be the people's fault but if the call was never sounded then he would be guilty. As can be seen in retrospect, Ezekiel did cry for his people to return to God with their hearts and reject the other gods that had crept into their lives. They did not obey.

In the book of 2 Timothy, the young Timothy, being groomed to be a leader of the people of God, was told that there was one purpose for the Word of God – *"that the man of God may be thoroughly equipped for every good work,"* and the way this happens is through, *teaching, rebuking, correcting and training in righteousness."*

In the middle of our broken cisterns, we find the church being led by paid, professional, full-time clergy. This relationship between pastor and congregation fosters an employer-employee bond rather than a follower-fellow follower bond. The ones being taught and led are actually the ones paying the leaders' salary. How could either side of this equation expect to be anything other than prejudiced? There is very little chance that the gospel minister will give the unadulterated Word of God because by its nature, the Word causes offense. When you add to this the fact that much of the congregation isn't even Christian, you wind up with an impossible situation. The "meat of the Word" regarding the things that are truly essential in our following of Jesus Christ must be taught but can't be taught because of the consequences. In this case, the fault needs to be laid at the feet of the ones who suffer because they are also the ones with the responsibility. Everything must be laid at the feet of the "watchmen on the wall." Huge sections of the Bible are being ignored because of denominational unbelief or prejudice by those charged with manning our pulpits.

If you are in a traditional fundamentalist church you have probably not heard a teaching on I Corinthians 12:1-11 in a long time because it talks about the manifestation of the Holy Spirit in the church and includes tongues. Even if a pastor believed that God had chosen to see His Spirit manifested in tongues, interpretation of tongues, prophecy, discerning of spirits, healing, word of wisdom, word of knowledge, faith and miracles he couldn't talk about them in church. If you are of a mainline, liturgical background, you are probably missing teachings on healing and miracles and if you are Pentecostal or charismatic, the emphasis is probably not on I Corinthians 11 that dissects the Lord's Supper or anything else that insinuates formality. Sincerely look at scripture without your preconceived notions and your denomination's statement of beliefs and you will find that we use the scriptural buffet line mentioned earlier to determine our doctrine and practices.

Each gospel minister is expected to follow the "party line" of his denomination and should he deviate from it he will face consequences. What if in his heart he realizes that the church is suffering because of his failure to give them the whole truth? What if he says, *"I've been wrong and I realize that there is more to our faith than we've thought"*

In defense of the loving men and women who are called to proclaim the gospel, if they begin to give the whole truth to the people they will probably lose their job, maybe their denominational affiliation and maybe even their career. In order to survive they many times compromise what they know in their own heart to be true. They hold back in order "to fight another day." I've done it! These things are allowed to happen because in our system it is possible for a person to walk in the church, be faithful to services for a few months, never profess faith in Jesus Christ that leads to repentance and before long be on committees and boards that determine the direction of the church. In many cases, people like this determine whether or not the truth is taught to the people. The denominational church opens its doors to Satan and then we wonder why the world around us is in the throws of sin. I have heard pastors say that they cannot speak out about homosexuality or abortion because of the disapproval of those in charge.

Consider a church where there is no professional clergy and all of the other gifts are functioning the way they should. There would still be a person that taught every week, whenever the body decided to meet. This person would be responsible for the spiritual maturity of the believers while others were concerned with the outreach of the church. The entire fellowship would visit those sick or in the hospital and nothing would be anyone's "job" but everything would be everyone's responsibility. If there was a failure, it would be that bodies' failure and there would be corporate repentance. If there was success then it would be the bodies' success and Christ would be magnified and exalted. The church would grow equally which is the organic way. We have created a hierarchy that appears to be leading but is really controlled by those who hold the pursestrings. Again I refer back to the church in *Acts 2:42-47* and believe that the same thing can happen today. We can really be a family fellowship caring more about each other than we care about ourselves.

Clergy need to be weaned off of the salaries that they have depended on for so long. They need to be out working like everybody else and using their gifts just like every one else. Out in the world is the greatest opportunity to grow and abound in the love of Jesus Christ and to have an influence on our world. They can find a job that offers the freedom to function according to the needs of the others in the fellowship. I am a real estate agent and our fellowship gives me money every week to take care of expenses and as my business grows, the money will decrease. We don't have a building or utility bills, I am the only expense other than our mission work but I don't want to be an expense, I want to be a servant and a blessing and want to be able to say whatever the Lord gives me to say; without fear of offence.

All of the gifts need to be developed by God right in the body where they belong. Leadership needs to be raised up right out of the congregation. Formal Christian education should not be a prerequisite for leadership as God has different ways of teaching different people. I saw this concept work especially well in Africa where we ministered to men that had become refugees from the war torn nation of Burundi. Our group was with them in Tanzania where they had escaped because of the tribal war between the Hutu's and Tutsi's. They had been called by God to serve the people but had no training. Each morning we would meet with them and have seminars that taught them the basics of being pastors. Having escaped war, the more we taught them the more we realized how strong their call was. God was grooming them to go back into Burundi where everyday their lives are in danger. The concept of a seminary education in circumstances such as these would be absurd. The day we ordained them was one of the most wonderful times I have ever spent as a Christian. I watched one man weep through the entire service as one of our team gave the charge. I could tell that this man had been given all of the education that he would ever need by the Holy Spirit who had been preparing him for this moment from before the foundation of the world.

Being led by such men can only mean that Christ's body on this planet has every resource needed to be a force.

These men were capable of anything God gave them not because of any teaching from us but simply by being His. This is the ideal.

Entertainment

If you were to ask most non-Christians what their mind picture of Christianity would be I think they would say a large room full of people with their hands raised with very emotional music loudly playing. If you asked about preaching they would most likely say a man in a suit, on a stage, walking back and forth, speaking in a loud voice, raising people up and then bringing them down emotionally. Ask about Christian media and you will hear about a pink haired lady and a white haired man, dressed in funny clothes, on a set that is made to look like "heaven" with guests who have funny hair and dress strange with lots of singing in-between.

I don't mean to be critical but please, tell me how we've gotten from a body of faithful, loving children of God to Hollywood. We broadcast this to the rest of the world and pervert the purity of simple saving faith in poor people around the world. Picture Jesus himself as a guest and you will surely realize the absurdity.

We are entertainment driven and our cisterns have taken on a theatrical air. Keep people entertained and you will keep people faithful. Worship is even described in terms of the music that is associated with it. Jesus talked of true worship to the woman at the well in Sychar and said, *"Believe me, woman, a time is coming when you will worship the Father neither on this mountain nor in Jerusalem... Yet a time is coming and has now come when the true worshipers will worship the Father in spirit and truth, for they are the kind of worshipers the Father seeks."* John 4:21&23 You and I live in this time! We, in order to truly worship, must worship in spirit and in truth.

That fact that "worship styles" could cause disagreement between children of God is a tragedy. Some people like to be very demonstrative and others do not. Some are very quiet, meditative and refined. Churches, fellowships break up over this silliness. People say, *"I'm going to go where I can worship longer or louder or quieter or contemporary or traditional."* The church no longer understands what worship is and we break up over it.

Jesus told the woman in Sychar that the time is now to worship *"in spirit and in truth." "Spirit"* is the Greek word, *"pneuma"* and in the context of these verses means, *"the element in man by which he perceives, reflects, feels and desires God."* God is the creator and giver of His Spirit within us. *"Truth,"* is *"alethia"* and means *"the reality pertaining to an appearance."* To put this all together in context, what Jesus was telling this woman was that in order to truly be worshipping God, we must be perceiving Him, reflecting Him, feeling Him and desiring Him, all the while appearing to the world to be exactly what we claim to be. What we claim to be are His children. This description could never just apply to the order of a meeting but communicates a lifestyle, a presence, the reality of the people of God on the earth ministering the love of Christ.

There is nothing wrong with coming together and praising the Lord, shouting, meditating, singing, as a matter of fact we are told to do this in *Ephesians 5:19, "speak to one another with psalms, hymns and spiritual songs. Sing and make music in your heart to the Lord."* We are in error if we call this worship, however; it is loving God completely on the inside and being real on the outside.

Entertainment and expressions of joy and emotion are wonderful but have nothing to do with real worship. If the style of music and emotional expression that we manifest when we come together divides us then we are not worshipping but are its antithesis. Instead of differences dividing us, they should bring the true church closer together because they are opportunities for us to put others needs and wants ahead of our own.

The American church has entertainment as its foundation rather than Christ and His saving power. Trying to attract people to Christ by bringing them pleasure will very seldom lead them to true repentance and his lordship because it is self centered. Christianity is not involved with self but with others. The early church saw the world be presented with the gospel through their lifestyle rather than their worship style and so must we.

The Lord's Supper

Probably the most critical perversion of Christ's directives to His disciples is in the celebration of the memorial feast commonly referred to as the Lord's Supper. The Apostle Paul in his first letter to the church at Corinth reproves the church by saying that their *"meetings do more harm than good."* They were partaking of the weekly feast in a manner that was not bringing glory to the Lord. *"When you come together, it is not the Lord's Supper you eat, for as you eat, each of you goes ahead without waiting for anybody else. One remains hungry, another gets drunk. Don't you have homes to eat and drink in? Or do you despise the church of God and humiliate those who have nothing? What shall I say to you? Shall I praise you for this? Certainly not!" I Corinthians 11:20-22*

The proper celebration of this feast was so important to the life of the church that Paul addresses it frankly and straightforward. The heart of what Christ instituted had been lost and Paul understood that the life of the body could not remain without the remembrance of Jesus' sacrifice.

> *"For I received from the Lord what I also passed on to you: The Lord Jesus, on the night he was betrayed, took bread, and when he had given thanks, he broke it and said, "This is my body, which is for you; do this in remembrance of me." In the same way, after supper he took the cup, saying, "This cup is the new covenant in my blood; do this, whenever you drink it, in remembrance of me." For whenever you eat this bread and drink this cup, you proclaim the Lord's death until he comes."*
>
> *(v23-26)*

He then begins to focus on what this body of believers is doing wrong in the supper. They were coming to eat the communion with sin in their lives. *"A man ought to examine himself before he eats the bread and drinks the cup." (v28)*

Two friends of mine were ministering in the central African nation of Burundi to pastors, teaching them the principles of leading God's people. One of the brothers was teaching on the Lord's Supper, talking about confession of sin and the mending of broken relationships as a prerequisite for partaking of the feast. When it came time to serve, they noticed people getting up and leaving the church. The teacher turned to the African bishop and said "Where is everybody going?" The bishop replied, "They are going to do what you said; they are going to mend their relationships." They gave the people time and then served the Supper. This is the true heart of what Jesus was instituting. It is still needed and is still at the heart of our gathering together.

Justin Martyr, second century Christian apologist, referred to communion or the "love feast" when talking about the way the early church came together.

"On the day called Sunday, all who live in cities or in the country gather together to one place, and the memoirs

*of the apostles or the writings of the prophets are read as long as time permits; then, when the reader has ceased, the president verbally instructs, and exhorts to the imitation of these good things. Then we all rise together and pray; and as we before said, **when our prayer is ended, bread and wine and water are brought, and the president in like manner offers prayers and thanksgivings, according to his ability, and the people assent, saying Amen.** And there is a distribution to each, and a participation of that over which thanks have been given; and to those who are absent a portion is sent by the deacons. And they who are well to do, and willing, give what each sees fit; and what is collected is deposited with the president, who succors the orphans and widows, and those who through sickness or any other cause are in want, and those who are in bonds, and the sojourner among us, and, in a word, takes care of all who are in need."*

In the very center of their fellowship was the celebration of remembrance; a renewal of the passion of the Lord, symbolically identified with by all those who have benefited from it. They were to surround it with love for God and for each other, forgiveness and giving. All of the true expressions of their faith were inextricably woven together in their gatherings, every week.

In the celebration of the first Lord's Supper, Jesus looked at twelve men whom He had lived in beautiful intimacy with for three years. He had taught them the essential elements of a walk with the Father and was preparing them for the time when He would no longer be with them. There needed to be a purging but in order for things to be removed, they must be revealed. In the breaking of the bread and the drinking of the cup Jesus "increases" and the individual "decreases." Just like the two disciples on the road to Emmaus in Luke 24, *"he took bread, and blessed it, and broke, and gave it to them. **And their eyes were opened, and they knew him;** and he vanished* *out of their sight." (v30b-31)* When Jesus is revealed to us there is a parallel revelation of what is inside of us and it must be dealt with. If believers' eyes really are opened and truly is accomplished in the proper remembrance of the sacrifice of Christ, then it must be allowed its efficacy.

When I was a boy living in Detroit, Michigan, my Dad would summon me for dinner with a loud whistle that everyone recognized. The whole neighborhood knew that he was calling Frankie home to supper and neighbors who realized that he was calling when I didn't, would let me know. Our heavenly Father calls us to a supper that is the essence of our corporate existence. Just as a family dinner is essential to the health of an earthly family, the Lord's Supper is vital to the children of God. It is the time for us to resolve differences, propagate love, receive vision and remember, simply remember.

There was a deeply spiritual element to the infant church that has been lost over the centuries. Theirs was a personal attitude of piety and devotion that translated to natural outreach in the daily affairs of life. What people tend to do over time is to be drawn towards one extreme or another. In our case these extremes are the emotionally demonstrative expressions of the Pentecostal/Charismatic movement or the deeply liturgical tone of Catholicism. What people tend to do naturally is to institutionalize their beliefs, formalizing what was heretofore natural. When the meeting of the church became formalized and governed, either of the manifestations of "worship syles" had to be "chosen" to one degree or another and made doctrinal; in truth there was no need to be anything other than what the Holy Spirit was leading the church to be. In any case, it can be stated that at the center of the meeting of the church was the Lord's Supper.

Chapter 12

Conclusion: The Meeting

"What then shall we say, brothers? When you come together, everyone has a hymn, or a word of instruction, a revelation, a tongue or an interpretation. All of these must be done for the strengthening of the church. If anyone speaks in a tongue, two – or at the most three – should speak, one at a time, and some one must interpret. If there is no interpreter, the speaker should keep quiet in the church and speak to himself and to God. Two or three of the prophets should speak, and the others should weigh carefully what is said. And if revelation comes to someone who is sitting down, the first speaker should stop. For you can all prophecy in turn so that everyone may be instructed and encouraged. The spirits of the prophets are subject to the control of the prophets. For God is not a God of disorder but of peace."
I Corinthians 14:26-33

In my heart is the picture of a group of Spirit led believers coming together for their weekly meeting. It is in a room at someone's home, maybe someone's office. All present are happy to be there, expectant, excited at what God is planning on doing. There is also a great joy in each life to see those whom they love so deeply and intimately.

As everyone gets quiet and contemplative and each becomes submissive to the Spirit, things start to happen. Someone begins to pray a message of worship to God. The Holy Spirit begins to "work the room" giving a message of adoration in tongues to the Lord to someone and to another the interpretation as in our Scripture. God responds by way of prophecy through another. The Spirit reveals direction for the Body. All present hear the "word of knowledge, God telling the family of faith exactly what is needed about the circumstances confronting them and another brings word of wisdom, what should be done with that knowledge. Needs arise; people bring up concerns and the Body ministers and prays, praying what the Spirit says to pray. Things happen and praise continues. God is worthy of honor and He is given it as part of His meeting with His people.

It is all about Him.

The works that are done in the lives of those in the Church are so that we will see Him, to magnify Him.

It is all about Him.

Paul told the people about the Lord's Supper as part of the meeting of the Church in I Corinthians 11: *"For whenever you eat this bread and drink this cup, you proclaim the Lord's death until He comes." (v26)*

It is all about Him. Everything is about Him.

The last verse in *I Corinthians 14, verse 40,* says: *"Let all things be done decently and in order." (KJV)*

What I have just described to you is decent and orderly. Nothing is done for self service, including miracles and healings; they are all just opportunities to see the glory of the Lord. God communicates His heart to His children and they respond in love and honor for Him, love for each other and love for the desperate world that they must soon return to. Isn't it beautiful? Isn't it all about Him?

A meeting such as this is the context of what was written earlier: the Holy spirit speaking to the Church. This is how the message was heard; through the Spirit speaking through the Body. We must hear Him again by getting rid of what has kept us from hearing and grabbing on to what He uses to speak to us.

We must smash our *"broken cisterns"* and come together to bask under the *"Fountan of Living Waters."* It will not be easy to give up what we have built but it will be worth it. The refreshment will immediately begin to invigorate us; we will come alive in Him and the world will see it – and many will want it.

There will still be programs but they won't be ours. We will be in the midst of the work of the Lord, His doing and everything will be happening before we even have a chance to label it; before we can put a name on it God will have already shown Himself and received His glory and men will be saved; countless men and women will be saved.

> *"And the Lord added to their number daily those who were being saved."*
> *Acts 2:47b*

Oh please, my Brothers and Sisters! Long for what I have described. I got it from the Word of God. Long for it and it will come! Cast off your *"cisterns, broken cisterns that can hold no water"* and stand instead under the *"Fountain of Living Waters."*

Appendix

The Dispensations of Scripture

Christians hear sermons and teachings every week that relate directly to the Holy Bible, the Word of God. One Sunday there might be a teaching from the ninth chapter of Daniel, teaching us about prayer and on Wednesday, there may be a message from I Corinthians that talks about order in the church. This is perfectly acceptable if it is not at the expense of the total revelation of scripture. Is the Bible simply a book of devotions from different sources that presents piety and devotion to the Lord from many different perspectives or is it more than that? Is it a unit with each word and phrase contributing to a greater message; a message that communicates the heart of God? The answer to the first question is "no" and to the second, "yes." We can see how to live a holy life through the study of God's word but its real point is to convey the heart of God that we might know Him, thereby falling in love with Him, thereby desiring to obey Him at every turn.

If the Bible really is a unit then we must ask what makes it such. What are the common threads through all of the books of the Bible? What pulls them all together? How do we *"rightly divide the word of truth"* as *II Timothy 2:15* directs us?

Christians do not generally know enough of the Word to contend for the faith. There should be a development towards maturity, a growth in our understanding of the One we worship. The usual growth of the believer consists of receiving Christ followed by a lifetime of fragmented messages designed to make us "a better person." Becoming a better person is not what this is all about. Through Christ we are "new creations" (*II Corinthians 5:17*) and simply need to learn to walk like what God has made us. Learning the character, traits and personality of God will inspire us and motivate us to walk spiritually rather than carnally, empowered by His grace. It is Him that we must learn!

We can't grow His character when we are only fed the "milk." A child who never graduates in his or diet will be unhealthy and in-turn unproductive. The Christian church should be full of believers in Christ who are growing in relationship with God AND knowledge of Him. As a matter of fact, relationship will grow as knowledge of Him grows.

In these few pages, we will explore the principles regarding the "right dividing" of His truth.

The Dispensations

Every student of the Bible needs to understand that there are basic principles of interpretation that must be adhered to consistently in order to *"rightly divide"* the Word. The most basic tenet of our study should be an understanding of **to whom** a passage is written. If I were to send you a letter directing you to a meeting place for this afternoon and someone else picks it up and reads the note next week, it will not be relevant to them. They are not to meet me but they can know that you and I met the week before.

When Paul writes to the church at Corinth, he addresses the letter *"To the church of God in Corinth, to those sanctified in Christ Jesus and called to be holy, together with those everywhere who call on the name of our Lord Jesus Christ – their Lord and ours." (1:2)*

He is specific about the people that are to directly understand that this letter is written to them. If you have called on the name of our Lord Jesus Christ then what he writes in this book are written directly to you and the rest of the church no matter when they live.

Look at the introduction to the book of James: *"... to the twelve tribes scattered among the nations." (v1)* James is written to Jewish believers in Christ who are scattered the world over, at any time. What is true of Christians in James is for us but when he is speaking to their Jewishness, it is not. How could it be when we are not all Jews?

Not all of the books in the Bible are letters with salutations that identify the readers; but we can still know to whom the book is written and to whom it applies. In Genesis Adam and Eve are told not to eat from the tree of the knowledge of good and evil. This doesn't apply to us because circumstances have changed. There is no tree of the knowledge of good and evil for us to be tempted with. You and I are not to sprinkle the blood of a lamb on our doorposts and lintels on the 14th of Nisan, every year, in order for the angel of death to pass over us, either. Our Lamb was Jesus and He was sacrificed once and for all; there is no need for us to go back to a practice that was for Israel, before Christ. The Passover is a wonderful memorial that should be understood by Christians and it is typical of the sacrifice of Christ that came later but it is not for us to practice.

How then do we determine what was written to us or for us and what was written to others. ***Dispensationalism*** takes the natural breaks in the history of God's dealings with mankind and interprets scripture based on them.

These are the dispensations:

Eden – *Gen 1:26* – *Gen 3:24* The period of time from the creation of man to his fall, in which he lived in the Garden of Eden. There was no knowledge of sin; innocence was its character with the only law being "*... but you must not eat from the tree of the knowledge of good and evil, for when you eat of it you will surely die." Genesis 2:17(KJV)* There was no curse for sin because sin did not exist and the true expression of love for God was wrapped up in this one prohibition. Love can only be expressed when there is a choice; we must choose to love and God gave man that choice. This dispensation began in *Genesis 2:15* and ended in *Genesis 3:24* with the reason being that man failed to obey. He was not able, in his own strength, to please God.

Before the Flood – the Antediluvian World – *Gen 4:1 – Gen 7:24* After Adam and Eve's banishment from the Garden, the conscience of man was left as the guiding force for love and obedience to God. Leaving man to his own devices is seen for the first time here as resulting in sin and destruction in the Flood, with God *"grieved that He had made man on the earth."* The sin that man progressed toward was of a particularly grievous sort and caused monumental catastrophe. Again, this period ended because of man's failure to obey God and defy His love but also ended in a covenant from God never to destroy the earth by water again..

After the Flood – The Post-diluvian World – When the waters of the Flood receded, God said to Noah, *"Bring out every kind of living creature that is with you – the birds, the animals, and all the creatures that move along the ground – so they can multiply on the earth and be fruitful and increase in number upon it." Genesis 8:17* and then in 9:1b, *"Be fruitful and increase in number and fill the earth."* First, the Lord tells Noah to send out the living creatures to fill the earth and then later tells him that human beings are to cover it also. God's intent is that mankind would cover the planet but instead what they wound up doing was *"... they found a plain in Shinar and settled there."* Again man is a failure in the ability to please God, being disobedient to His wishes.

The Patriarchs – Beginning with Abraham, God dealt with people in family units with the head of the family, the patriarch, being the priest. This period is marked by the covenant between Abraham and God and later Isaac and Jacob and God. The Semitic line (descending from Shem) became the people that God was "choosing" to show Himself to the world. Abraham is the beginning of the Hebrews, the nation of Israel. This dispensation ended the same as the others – in disobedience, in Egypt.

The Law – While Jacob's family, the Hebrews, were in captivity, God built them in number and kept them segregated and then, after 430 years, He led them out at Moses hand. Leading them through the desert, God gave them the law by which they were now subject. They would be guided in their devotion to the Lord by a sacrificial system and a series of laws that addressed every area of their life. Until the coming of Christ and His offer of redemption to the Jews, the law was in effect. No human being was able to keep God's law but in addition to being a standard by which man was to live, it had another purpose.

> *"What, then, was the purpose of the law? It was added because of transgressions until the Seed* (Christ) *to whom the promise was referred had come."*
>
> *Galatians 3:19*
>
> *"Before this faith came* (faith in Christ), *we were held prisoners by the law, locked up until faith should be revealed. So the law was put*

*in charge **to lead us to Christ that we might be justified by faith**. Now that faith has come, we are no longer under the supervision of the law."*
Galatians 3:23-25

Jesus fulfilled the law; He kept it and paid all of its requirements, making possible a personal relationship with the Father through acceptance of the Son. This completed the Law! Freedom and peace could now reign in the hearts of those who would but believe. There could now be the intimacy between God and man that had been missing since Adam's sin. The dispensation of the law was the preparation time for the offering of the kingdom to Israel and all mankind. What we know to be true, however, was that He was rejected; He was nailed to a tree and rejected! Even in this rejection, man's salvation was won. Even though this dispensation ended in failure, like all the others, man's redemption was purchased.

The Church – This is the dispensation that this book focuses on. At the day of Pentecost, the Jewish Feast of Weeks, when many pilgrims were in Jerusalem, the Holy Spirit descended on Jesus' disciples. He had told them to *"tarry at Jerusalem for the promise of the Father, which you have heard of me."*

> *"When the day of Pentecost came, they were all together in one place. Suddenly a sound like the blowing of a violent wind came from heaven and filled the whole house where they were sitting. They saw what seemed to be tongues of fire that separated and came to rest on each one of them. All of them were filled with the Holy Spirit and began to speak in other tongues as the Spirit enabled them."*
> *Acts 2:1-4*

This is the record of the birth of the church. A dispensation began that would be marked by the indwelling of the Holy Spirit in those who would confess Jesus as Lord. They would be bound together as the church. Paul called it the *"body of Christ"* and the *"building fitly framed."* The church would be the literal presence of Christ on the earth and minister through the gifts that He would give to its individual members. Every gift was necessary and would result in manifestations of the power of the Holy Spirit through Christians. The Lord told His twelve closest disciples that, *"I tell you the truth, anyone who has faith in me will do what I have been doing. He will do even greater things than these, because I am going unto the Father."* John 14:12

There was to be a power lived that would show the glory of the Lord and the way of salvation to all mankind. All the tools are in place, all of the needs are obvious for the church to impact the "lostness" of the world.

The church age is a parenthetical period of time in which Israel is still at the heart of God's plan to reach mankind. The Jews and Gentiles are, for a time, brought together in one body to be the people of God. This dispensation will end the same as all of the others, in failure of mankind to accept Christ's offer and the necessity of God to introduce another way to present truth to mankind. Christ will be returning for His church at the end of this dispensation in an event termed the "rapture" described in *I Thessalonians 4:13-18*:

"Brothers, we do not want you to be ignorant about those who fall asleep, or to grieve like the rest of men, who have no hope. We believe that Jesus died and rose again and so we believe that God will bring with Jesus those who have fallen asleep in him. According to Jesus' own word, we tell you that we who are still alive, who are left till the coming of the Lord, will certainly not precede those who have fallen asleep. For the Lord himself will come down from heaven, with a loud command, with the voice of the archangel and

with the trumpet call of God, and the dead in Christ will rise first. After that, we who are still alive and are left will be caught up together with them in the clouds to meet the Lord in the air. And so we will be with the Lord forever. Therefore encourage each other with these words."

After the removal by Christ of His church, Israel will again be the vehicle by which the world will hear of God's redemption. This time is marked by the leadership of a false "messiah," the *Antichrist*, who will lead humanity in unbelief, idolatry and rebellion during a time called the tribulation.

The Tribulation – This is a seven year window of time in which the influence of the church is removed and man is once again left to his own devices. There will be a supremely evil world ruler who will wield influence over all of humanity, the Antichrist, and will forge a coalition of other smaller political and religious influences. Israel has a change of heart, the blinders come off and they accept Jesus as the Messiah and the earth is given the chance to believe in Christ through the witness of 144,000 Jewish evangelists. Through terrible calamity and the obvious polarization of good and evil, the world chooses. However, too much of the earth makes the wrong choice and there is a final horrible battle in which Christ comes to the rescue of the chosen people and the believers of the world. The *battle of Armageddon* leads to Christ returning again this time to rule and reign. He will set foot upon the Mount of Olives and take up the reins of His kingdom for a thousand years.

The Millenium - The thousand year reign of Christ is characterized by peace over the entire planet. It is a time in which Israel is the head of all the nations and whose tumultuous national existence ends and peace is established. Satan and his angels are bound in chains and have no influence upon men. It will be seen that man still has the elements in his nature to reject God as even without Satan's temptations, some will still not believe. There will be no excuse for anyone to say that Satan made them do it.

Near the end of the thousand years, Satan is loosed from his bondage and allowed to tempt as before but will be overcome in a final battle in which he is permanently dealt with being cast in the *Lake of Fire* at the *Great White Throne Judgment*. This is the judgment in which all of the believers and unbelievers other than the pre tribulation church are judged.

The New Jerusalem – The final age is the end of all ages; where man lives in perfection with all of the beauty of the Garden of Eden restored. Perfect communion between God and man is the norm with no chance of it ever being lost. This is "heaven;" what everyone had always hoped would be. It is what Jesus died for. Time will be no more. Our corruption, our bodies that are affected by the laws of thermodynamics, will be no more. We will not age and our mortality, the fact that we are ravaged by time will end. (I Corinthians 15)

Interpretation

Scripture is a total, a unit. It is not 66 independent books on the same subject but an interdependent compilation of revelation that, when fitted together, gives one clear, concise message concerning the redemption of man. Every word of it is written **for** everyone and **to** someone. As discussed earlier, we must know who a passage is addressing in order to know who is to obey. Dispensational interpretation gives us an orderly way of doing this. We are able to look at the time period that the text is written and who it is written to and know whether it speaks of Israel, the Gentiles or the church of Christ. This is imperative in Biblical studies and to an understanding of this book. Jesus came to die and be raised again to usher in an age of power and might; an age in which mankind would see God through His works in His people. The conditions that existed in the entire history of the people of God would come to a pinnacle, a zenith through the Church; broken cisterns would be shattered and cast away and we would return to the fountain of living waters.